Vow of Prosperity

Spiritual Solutions for Financial Freedom

Noel Jones and Scott Chaplan

DESTINY IMAGE® PUBLISHERS, INC.
P.O. Box 310, Shippensburg, PA 17257-0310

*"Speaking to the Purposes of God for this Generation
and for the Generations to Come."*

This book and all other Destiny Image, Revival Press, Mercy Place, Fresh Bread, Destiny Image Fiction, and Treasure House books are available at Christian bookstores and distributors worldwide.

For a U.S. bookstore nearest you, call 1-800-722-6774.
For more information on foreign distributors, call 717-532-3040.
Or reach us on the Internet: www.destinyimage.com.

ISBN 10: 0-7684-2488-7
ISBN 13: 978-0-7684-2488-1

For Worldwide Distribution, Printed in the U.S.A.

1 2 3 4 5 6 7 8 9 10 11 / 09 08 07

Endorsement

Scott Chaplan has served as General Counsel for Hayward Lumber Company since 1991. Scott's advice and friendship—both personally and for our company—have proven invaluable, and he has contributed greatly to our continued growth and success. Scott and Bishop Jones have a firm grasp on triple bottom line investing, and Bethany Square is a testament to their core values of improving the world one neighborhood at a time. *Vow of Prosperity* encapsulates their mutual quest to educate, empower, and free everyone desirous of prosperity.

William E. Hayward
CEO, Hayward Lumber Company (est. 1919)
Chairman, Forest Stewardship Council (FSC)

Table of Contents

If You Have It, Work It!

In this book you will be given many truths that will help you discover prosperity in every area of your life. But in order for that to happen, you will have to draw on the talents that God has given you to make your life work. The gifts are given for a reason. Not only to bless God, but for you to be blessed by the gracious gift of God and then extend that blessing to others.

Your faithfulness in handling what God has given to you will determine your success. To make a "Vow of Prosperity" means that you make a commitment to take your gifts that have been given by the God of all grace and employ those gifts in the opportunities that He will bring your way.

The proven successful principles you will read about in the following pages can only work for you as you put your trust and faith in Him, and allow the gifts to be activated in your life in such a way that you will bring profit to the Lord. To the degree that you are faithful, then more will be given to you.

Distilled to its essence, this book is designed to open the door to spiritual solutions for your financial freedom.

PARABLE OF THE TALENTS

Jesus was a master at communicating spiritual truth by using a variety of effective ways—aphorisms, parables, and even His miracles were methods of instruction. The use of the parable was His favorite way to deliver heavenly truths.

> *For the kingdom of Heaven is as a man travelling into a far country, who called his own servants, and delivered unto them his goods. And unto one he gave five talents, to another two, and to another one; to every man according to his several ability; and straightway took his journey.*

> *Then he that had received the five talents went and traded with the same, and made them other five talents. And likewise he that had received two, he also gained other two. But he that had received one went and digged in the earth, and hid his lord's money.*

> *After a long time the lord of those servants cometh, and reckoneth with them. And so he that had received five talents came and brought other five talents, saying, Lord, thou deliveredst unto me five talents: behold, I have gained beside them five talents more.*

> *His lord said unto him, Well done, thou good and faithful servant: thou hast been faithful over a few things, I will make thee ruler over many things: enter thou into the joy of thy lord.*

> *He also that had received two talents came and said, Lord, thou deliveredst unto me two talents: behold, I have gained two other talents beside them.*

> *His lord said unto him, Well done, good and faithful servant; thou hast been faithful over a few things, I will make thee ruler over many things: enter thou into the joy of thy lord.*

Then he which had received the one talent came and said, Lord, I knew thee that thou art an hard man, reaping where thou hast not sown, and gathering where thou hast not strawed: And I was afraid, and went and hid thy talent in the earth: lo, there thou hast that is thine.

His lord answered and said unto him, Thou wicked and slothful servant, thou knewest that I reap where I sowed not, and gather where I have not strawed: Thou oughtest therefore to have put my money to the exchangers, and then at my coming I should have received mine own with usury. Take therefore the talent from him, and give it unto him which hath ten talents.

For unto every one that hath shall be given, and he shall have abundance: but from him that hath not shall be taken away even that which he hath (Matthew 25:14-29).

This is one of the classic parables of Jesus that illustrates a timeless truth. The picture He paints with His words illustrates the dynamic reality that God has given talents to each of us. He equips us for our lives—here and there. The utilization of His gifts blesses us here, and rewards us there.

In discussing the issue of gifts, there is a question that will arise periodically and ultimately: What did you do with the gifts of God?

It isn't just a question for those who stood under the sway of His words. In the talents parable Jesus is reaching out and talking to all people. Through this parable Jesus still speaks to us in our postmodern world. The eschatological placement of the parable tells us that this question will not go unasked at the significant times in our lives, particularly at the end of it. The question will always haunt us.

The interesting thing that I have discovered is that often God will use the situations of life to ask us this question over and over again. Will God allow the circumstance of my life to question me about if and how I am using His gifts? Yes, the demand of life is gong to force us to reach for every gift God gives. God allows for this demand to exist to align us properly to our destiny.

It is quite evident that often our pain comes as a result of not having walked in the gifts of God. The introductory word to the parable is "for," and in the Greek is *gar*. It can be interpreted as "you see" or "it is exactly like." This parable is not separated from the Parable of the Servant (Matt. 24:45-51) and the Parable of the Bridesmaids (Matt. 25:1-13). They are connected in Jesus' train of thought. Matthew chapter 25 verse 14 ends these two parables with these words: "*Watch therefore, for ye know neither the day nor the hour wherein the Son of man cometh.*"

The message in the parable of the virgins is about *waiting*, while in the parable of the talents it is about *working*. Both are talking about watchfulness and being prepared, but one focuses on "waiting" for the Lord, while it is here displayed in "working" for Him. Jesus combines the inward spiritual life with its external activity.

The direct meaning of *talent* is monetary, however; it may be interpreted as "work." *Talent* has been transliterated into the English language as a name of a personal gift or *aptitude*.[1] This can be a valuable way to discover one's responsibility before God. The work you are gifted to do is a gift of grace.

The excitement of the saint is to find what God has gifted you to do. When you make this discovery you will have greater wisdom to know how to plot out your life. Your work may be small to you, but it is immensely integral to the purposes of God. How we use grace determines destiny. Your destiny is attached to your discovery and use of the gift.

Your Attitude Toward the Gift

> *To one he gave five talents, to another two, to another one—to* **each according to his individual capacity;** *and then started from home.* **Without delay** *the one who had received the five talents went and* **employed them in business, and gained** *five more. In the same way he who had the two gained two more* (Matthew 25:15-17 Weymouth New Testament, emphasis added).

> *To one he gave five talents, to another two, and to another one; to each* **according to his respective ability,** *and immediately set out. Then he who had received the five talents,* **went and traded with them, and gained** *other five. Likewise he who had received two, gained other two* (Matthew 25:15-17 Living Oracles New Testament, emphasis added).

Immediately, without delay means that the servant takes whatever the Lord has given him and instantly goes to work with enthusiasm. "I am so glad I have this gift. I must now use it!" From the depths of an appreciative heart toward the Giver, the servant wastes no time creating a profit for his master. It is the excitement of an eager faith.

Immediately is followed by three verbs: moved out, went to work, and won. These are all aggressive words. The power of your blessing is not in your passivity, but in your activity. They got going. They got working. They got profit. There is an intensity of movement in the actions of the servants.

It's been explained that waiting for the Lord is not for Matthew a fact of religious inwardness nor of a unique fervor nor even of prayer. It is an active engagement that mobilizes the believer in the invitation to risky initiatives.

The only passivity is in the grace of the gift. Grace precedes work. Words do not lead to grace. It is the servant's respect for the Giver that motivates him to utilize the gift to the maximum. Your zeal to optimize your gifts, expresses in direct proportion, your appreciation of the Giver's sacrifice. We did not earn the gifts, but we gain the rewards of the gifts, and thus give glory to the Giver. We receive the gifts, and we give the Giver glory.

The strength of faith is exhibited in the intensity by which one works. It corroborates James' declaration that, "Even so faith, if it hath not works, is dead, being alone" (James 2:17).

Such a faith is dead in the sense that it is ineffectual, inefficient, and inadequate. (See Romans 7:8; Hebrews 6:1, 9:14). The phrase *heautou,* placed at the conclusion of the clause for emphasis, modifies the word "faith" and not the word "dead" (faith alone, KJV; faith by itself, RSV).

The word *heautou* means "by itself, on its own," and describes a faith that is not merely outwardly inoperative but inwardly dead. A faith without works (by itself) is no more a living faith than a corpse without breath is a living person. "It cannot stand alone and be of any avail. Only when it shows its power in works is it of the slightest value."[2]

Faith and works go together as life and breath, and the former cannot exist without the latter. The professed believer who refrains from helping those in need exhibits the type of behavior that is associated with one whose faith is dead—ineffectual and make-believe.

So the one who has received the gift and has faith, will use the gift and manifest faith in the Giver by activating the gift in service for Him.

"What shall we render to God for all of His benefits...?" We will do something with the gifts He has given us. Since we know we have something to use, we will use it. We immediately upon discovery, move out, work it, and win.

How shall we view the talented but unfaithful servant? He had no thrill to be gifted as he was. Notice the difference—aggressive verbs were used for the servants given the ten and the two, and recessive verbs were used for the servant given one talent.

BURYING A GIFT

Notice the comparison:

- The two faithful servants:
  Moved out, worked it and won others.

- The faithless servant:
  Went away, dug a hole, and buried it.

The attitude toward the Giver now becomes evident in the response to the gift by the faithless servant—he dug a hole. How many holes have you dug because of the attitudes of others toward your visions? How many holes have you dug because of your low self-esteem? How many holes have you dug because of your friends' opinions of your vision? How many holes have you dug because of your past failures, ones that you think will haunt you forever? How many holes have you dug because of your family's judgment of your abilities to succeed?

It is one thing to dig a hole, but when we bury the gift, the action carries a sense of permanence. Now you have to dig another hole to release your gift. However, before you dig the hole to unbury the gift, you must determine where you buried it.

How often has it happened that you could not even *find* the gift because you buried it so long ago or so deeply that you lost it? Have you ever hidden something from yourself so well that you could not find it again? Have you done that with your gifts because of your fears? Have you done that because of your concept of God?

GIFTS AND REWARDS

In the parable, after a long time the lord of those servants returned and settled his accounts with them. At some point everyone's opportunities, as well as the character of his life and works, will be considered and rewarded accordingly. When the Lord sees your faithfulness regarding how you have handled your gifts, you will hear these words: "Well done, good and faithful servant; thou hast been faithful over a few things, I will make thee ruler over many things: enter thou into the joy of thy lord" (Matt. 25:23).

ENDNOTES

1. Fausett's Bible Dictionary, from Theophilos Digital Bookcase, © 1998, International Bible Translators.

2. B.W. Johnson's New Testament Commentary, from Theophilos Digital Bookcase, © 1998, International Bible.

Spiritual Solutions
for Financial Freedom

CHAPTER ONE

Keys to Personal and Financial Success

MOST PEOPLE HAVE A DREAM of the possibilities created by a prosperous life. We imagine the advantages that will come our way if we could attain that dream. The problem is that few people are willing to go through the process that leads them to the fulfillment of their dreams. Many want to become the next great Bishop T.D. Jakes, Joyce Meyer, or Bishop Eddie Long, the next Oprah Winfrey or Jada Pinckett, Bill Gates, Denzel Washington, Will Smith, Venus or Serena Williams, Tavis Smiley, or Warren Buffett. Dreams are important, but if they are not accompanied by a commitment to the process, dreams will continue to be daydreams and you will never enjoy a dream come true.

It is easy to look at those who have succeeded and wish that we could be like them; but the one thing that is common to all successful people is that they were willing to endure the required process to attain their dreams. Their success is the result of hard work, discipline, risk taking, maintained motivation—and they did not take "no" for an answer. Success didn't happen for them overnight. There are always struggles and obstacles that await those who want to succeed in life.

CATHY HUGHES – MRS. RADIO

Cathy Hughes is an African-American entrepreneur, radio and television personality, and business executive. In the world of radio and business, she has built an empire and attained status of truly heroic proportions.

Like most successful people, the pathway to the top was not an easy road. A college dropout who became pregnant at age 16, Hughes gained 82 pounds and suffered from depression. However, her son, Alfred, became her inspiration and her motivation. She slept nights in a sleeping bag on the radio station's floor and played her own LPs brought from home to fill airtime—she has worked in every aspect of radio from sales to talk show host.

After working for KOWH, Hughes was offered a job as a lecturer at the School of Communications at Howard University in Washington, D.C. In 1975, she became general manager of the university's radio station.

In 1979, Hughes founded Radio One, using her earnings to buy AM radio station WOL in Washington, D.C. After the previous employees had destroyed the facility, she had to start from square one. She lost her home and had to move with her young son into the radio station building. She took a gamble and changed the R&B format to a 24-hour talk format. Even her Black supporters thought she was crazy.

"They told me Black people wouldn't listen to talk radio," she recalls. "During those days, we got as many complaints from listeners as we did from advertisers that Black folks could not talk, that it was embarrassing to the race."

Today, Hughes and her son, Alfred Liggins, III, president and CEO, work side by side running Radio One, Inc., the largest African-American owned and operated broadcast company in the nation.

In May 1999, Hughes and Liggins took their company public. Hughes made history again by becoming the first African-American woman with a company on a major stock exchange. Radio One's market cap currently exceeds $2 billion.

In 2000, *Black Enterprise* named Radio One "Company of the Year," *Fortune* magazine rated it one of the "100 Best Companies to Work For," and Radio One was inducted into the Maryland Business Hall of Fame.

Hughes' passion has paid off. Today, this hardworking, hands-on entrepreneur is sitting atop a multibillion dollar enterprise that includes 70 radio stations in nine of the top 20 markets for African-American listeners. She is the most powerful woman in radio and heads a business that she built from scratch—one listener, one employee, one community project, and one radio station at a time.

In January 2004, Radio One launched TV One, a national cable and satellite television network which bills itself as the "lifestyle and entertainment network for African-American adults." Hughes interviews prominent African-Americans for the network's talk program, "TV One on One."[1]

INSTANT SUCCESS IS A MYTH

The sacrifices involved in fulfilling your dream of success can be exacerbating. There will be opposition and setbacks. There will be failure and disappointment. The promise of instant success is a myth. There are few, if any, overnight successes in real life. Winning the lottery cannot be counted as instant success. The statistics of lottery winners who lost everything after only a year or two are staggering.

There is much learned in the process that will sustain you after you reach your goals. Success does not come by *waiting* for it. It comes by *working* for it. Too many people are waiting for a miracle to drop in their laps.

Living in the fantasy world of expected instant success will be a great hindrance to reaching your desired dream. You must start the journey understanding that no good thing comes without a price. You must be willing to walk through the pain and rejection. You must understand that *failure is never final*; it is simply a part of the process on the journey.

No one makes it overnight, and those who do usually fail. Why? Because they have never been trained to manage success, spend sensibly, and invest wisely. What invariably happens when they get their first real taste of money is self-destructive. Because they have no plan about how to handle success, they end up losing what they gained.

Attitudes of the Successful

"If I could just get a new exotic car, a mansion, or had mad amounts of diamond and gold jewelry, then I know I'd live happily ever after." Your motivation will determine your success. Money is not a goal. It is a byproduct of reaching your goal. A vast majority of actors and actresses go to school, work hard, and take whatever job they can while striving toward their goal. Their goal is to perform in the movies, on stage or television—money is the byproduct. An athlete will work in the gym, manage his diet, and work endlessly at developing his skill so he can ultimately play in the National Football League. The NFL is the goal—money is the byproduct.

Money cannot be your motivation. That motivation will not sustain you through the difficult times. Your contribution to society is your goal, and money simply becomes the reward of all of your hard labor. Successful people want to accomplish something in life. Their eyes are not on the luxuries that fame will bring them. Their eyes are on the goal of succeeding in life. They understand that wealth is the byproduct of accomplishment.

This is why it is dangerous to become rich overnight. You never had to work for the wealth. You never had a goal in mind. You were never focused on a particular dream. You never had to work, or save, or face failure—and you didn't have the opportunity to build character through the process.

What you gain overnight, you are bound to lose overnight. Although God can and often does get people out of debt overnight, it is not necessarily the best method for everyone. People need to discover what got them into enormous debt in the first place. If you freely increase your personal debt by careless use of credit cards, you must learn that the way back is a long arduous road. It can be accomplished; but you must make sacrifices in order to reach the goal of getting out of debt. It is important to understand what to *embrace* and what to *avoid*. Learning when to buy and when to refrain from purchasing is part of the process.

Ask Oprah, Bill Gates, Denzel Washington, or even Tiger Woods how they are enjoying their "overnight success." If you read their life stories, you will discover that their journeys to success were long and hard. You don't build an empire in a day.

Winning the Masters golf tournament was not a stroke of luck for Tiger Woods. As a young kid he lived under the discipline his father provided. He spent hours, days, months and years stroking the ball. While others his age were hanging out, he was sacrificing, working, and perfecting his game. He is now the undisputed best golfer in the game. His success was no accident.

Successful people make a *decision* about what they want in life. Then they are *determined* and *disciplined* in working toward their goal. Successful people appreciate and embrace rather than despise or avoid the process.

THE PROCESS CREATES APPRECIATION FOR SUCCESS

I've been preaching and traveling for the past 35 years. I know that may surprise you, but I started out early in life. If I had back then what I have now, it would have been disastrous. I would have been reckless and irresponsible. I would not have had an infrastructure set in place to be able to accommodate and appreciate what I have right now. Going through the process gave me a greater appreciation for everything that I now have.

It took time for me to gain the wisdom that I have, and to appreciate the value of everything that God has given me. When I was very young, it took time for me to process the heavy realization of the gifts that I was blessed with. The process included pain and rejection, and did I enjoy that? No! But I now understand that there is no success without heartache and failure.

Many people try everything they can to avoid the process of life. They look for shortcuts to success. They don't understand that shortcuts only lead down dark alleys and toward dead ends. Look at those who get involved with dealing drugs. They have avoided the pathway of education and have chosen the "quick fix." Most drug dealers are entrepreneurs and very smart people. They have simply chosen a dangerous shortcut to success—a shortcut that eventually leads to jail or premature death.

Unfortunately, they don't want to go through the process of becoming skilled Chief Executive Officers of major corporations, or entrepreneurs, or even designers. Many of them would be phenomenal pharmacists or even medical doctors. After all, they enjoy selling the stuff. But they view the process of going through years of college or applied training and study as not being worth their while, or even worth the wait. They have been sold on the "bling bling" life of financial riches and security, but refuse to take the legal path to arrive at that place. They see the cars, houses, and status, and want it overnight. The quick route is the more appealing way. Little do they realize that the quick route, the instant path, will land them in a lonely dark cell.

Great musicians and rappers go through a process before they arrive at their blessing. They have to practice long hours perfecting their skills and craft. In their early days they had to play, sing, or rap wherever and whenever they could to get exposure and gather an audience. They justified the time put in as "paying my dues." When you pay your dues you have a greater appreciation for the reward at the end of the rainbow. Many of them held down 9-to-5 jobs while pursuing their passion and caring for the needs of their households. Some of them made demo CDs and sold them out of the trunk of their cars at supermarkets, malls, movies theatres, churches, and wherever to get their work out to the public.

To Possess the Promise You Must Go Through the Process

There is definitely a process that everyone has to endure in order to possess the promise. The question—how badly do you really want to reach your goal, to possess your dream and His promise? What are you willing to go through in order to get what God said is yours? Is the journey worth it, or is it just too laborious?

You must answer these questions honestly before you move forward. If the promise is really worth it to you, then you will go through the process gracefully knowing that on the other end of your wilderness experience is the Promised Land.

Young preachers want to become like me overnight. While that may be somewhat flattering to me, it really does not make sense at all. If people want what I have, then they must first walk in my shoes. They must go through what I've gone through. It is not just about getting my tapes, listening to them, and practicing how to mimic me. You may learn style and approach that way, but you won't learn the lessons that I learned that shaped my fundamental philosophy and fashioned my life in such a way that I now have something to say.

Although I am enrolled in the lifelong process of learning— I read books, periodicals, magazines, and journals voraciously— there are still some things that only come through experience. You may argue with my theology all day long because you don't see things the way I see them. You may have been educated in a different stream of learning from me that may oppose what I've learned and how I've been trained. Our arguing some fine point would be utterly foolish and most unproductive, because you cannot refute my *testimony* which is derived from my *experience*.

My experience validates my ministry and my mission. Although some may have several doctorate degrees and designations, they still need experience. If I tell you that the Jesus of the Gospels healed the sick and raised the dead, you can argue that point till hell freezes over, if you don't believe in divine healing.

On the other hand, if I tell you that Jesus healed me on my deathbed and raised me up to tell you about it, there is nothing substantial that you can say or do to rebut my claim. It's through life's processes that we gather the experience that gives us something to talk about. Take that away and all you have is a systematic theology. Add experience to that, and you have the power of God. Without experience, all of our knowledge simply puffs us up and makes us appear larger than we really are.

It's not about the custom clothing, or the Louis Vuitton briefcase, or the alligator shoes. Those are just outward trappings that do not necessarily mean you have anything to offer. What really matters are the stories about how you had to preach and did not have a briefcase, but rather a plastic bag, in which to carry your Bible and sermon notes.

When you tell me about the time when the shoes you wore had holes in them, or perhaps you did not even have a decent pair of shoes to wear at all—that's experience. How about when you had to borrow a suit just to go to the job interview, and your uncle had to loan you his necktie, yet today you own your own clothing line? *That's* the process that you cannot avoid. It is all part of the *making process*, the process that prepares you for your reward.

We will close this chapter with two more great stories of success that will give you strength for your own journey.

Valerie Daniels-Carter – Restaurant Queen

After years of struggle, hard work, and even tragedy, Valerie Daniels-Carter has found her dream reaping the benefits of a strong work ethic and faith in God. As President and

CEO of the country's largest African-American-owned restaurant franchise, holding company, Valerie Daniels-Carter and her brother, John Daniels, a lawyer, own V & J Foods Holding Companies Inc., which controls 96 Pizza Huts and 41 Burger Kings throughout the Midwest and New York.

Daniels-Carter received a Bachelor of Arts degree from Lincoln University and went on to receive a Master's in business administration degree from Milwaukee's Cardinal Stritch College.

Her dream began in 1984 when she opened her first Burger King restaurant in Milwaukee, Wisconsin. With little knowledge about the fast-food industry, the entrepreneur took two years to learn the ropes prior to starting her first franchise. After she was confident with her developing management skills, Daniels-Carter opened her second restaurant a year later and the third one soon after.

She has been instrumental in the development and implementation of numerous community projects, including the Daniels-Carter Youth Center and Jeffrey A. Carter Sr. Center for Community Empowerment and Family Reunification. She consistently provides relief to the distressed by supplying basic necessities to families in need due to unforeseen circumstances, and she partners with prison ministries by assisting families of incarcerated individuals.

While her business blossomed, Daniels-Carter had to overcome the loss of two important people in her life. In 1999 her husband died in an accident. The following year, her mother passed away. Through it all, she maintained her vigorous lifestyle, while acquiring awards and recognition. She does all this while reminding herself and others, "Don't allow anyone or anything to prevent you from achieving excellence."

"If you would have asked me in 1982, when I first started my application process, whether or not I thought I would have 98 restaurants in 1997, I probably would have said, 'Heck, I'm just happy to get one.' But it's an evolving industry, and I don't ever say 'can't, never, or no.'"

"My faith in God has kept me with the wherewithal and the energy to move forward. I don't put my faith in money. I put my faith in God, because money can be here today and gone tomorrow. I recognize that I'm not where I am because I'm great, but I am where I am because God has just gifted me and blessed me, and I don't take that for granted."[2]

THE PURSUIT OF HAPPINESS

A blockbuster movie released in 2006, *The Pursuit of Happyness*[3], illustrates the point perfectly. Will Smith played the character of Chris Gardner. Chris Gardner in real life was an out-of-work salesman in San Francisco who won custody of his young son just as he was about to start a new job. In the beginning all does not go well for Gardner in his pursuit of happiness. He ends up in a homeless shelter trying to look after his son.

In 1983 he spent many nights in homeless shelters and sometimes lived on the streets. On some nights he and his son would crash at flophouses or hole up in a far corner of Union Square. Bathing was often done in the sinks of public bathrooms. For meals, Gardner took his son, then a toddler, to the soup kitchen at Glide Memorial Church.

But he did not give up on his dream. It was in that soup kitchen where he met the Rev. Cecil Williams. Williams allowed Gardner to keep his son at the soup kitchen until he finally received a $1,000-a-month paycheck as a stockbroker trainee. He eventually saved enough money to put down a deposit on a rental house in Berkeley, California. After years of hard work and determination, Gardner became an extremely wealthy man owning his own brokerage firm. He did not take the shortcut offered to him on the streets. He took the high and hard road that led to true and lasting success.

ENDNOTES

1. http://www.blackperspective.com/pages/mag_articles/sum01_soulofthecity.html; http://www.tv-one.tv/shows/show.asp?sid=123&id=1126.

2. http://blackentrepreneurshalloffame.blogspot.com/2005/08/valerie-daniels-carter.html; http://www.qsrmagazine.com/articles/interview/90/Daniels-Carter-2.phtml

3. "The Pursuit of Happyness," Sony Pictures, 2006.

CHAPTER TWO

What Is Prosperity?

This is a very short chapter, but it might be one of the most important. Why? Because you will have to determine for yourself what prosperity is. Your definition will then determine the goals and vision for your life. To begin with, prosperity is not relegated to the accumulation of material wealth. Gandhi was not a wealthy man, though through his struggle and the disciplined, relentless application of passive resistance, he led his people and changed the world. Mother Teresa was not nor did she ever strive to accumulate wealth, but the prosperity derived from her lifelong mission painted an indelible mark on the fabric of humanity and set the bar for others to strive toward in terms of giving, kindness, altruism, and love.

Prosperity means "a successful, flourishing or thriving condition." Webster defines it as "good fortune." A teacher with energetic, happy students hungry for knowledge is prosperous, and prosperous is a parent admired by a well-raised, happy child. Your vision, translated into tangible goals will define prosperity for you, and your achievement of those goals in a manner that satisfies you means prosperity in your life. Is the unhappy billionaire prosperous? How about the drug-addicted musician with platinum albums and no family or true friends?

How do you define prosperity? Answer that question honestly before you read on. Remember, we can't reach goals we don't set, and we can't set goals we don't understand. Approach the goal of defining prosperity for yourself holistically, and encompass your mental, spiritual, and physical welfare in your analysis. Sustainable prosperity requires balance, and your prosperity tripod requires all three legs to maintain balance.

The Law of Attraction states that "like attracts like." Look at your life. What and who you are surrounded by determines what you have attracted to your life. This is one of the keys to prosperity. Your spirit will either attract negatively or positively. We are all like magnets. We tend to create our own reality by the things to which we give attention.

If we focus on negative things, we will get negative things. If we are negative, we will attract negative people into our lives and facilitate the growth of negativity. We attract those things in our lives (money, relationships, business opportunities) that we focus on. When we focus on our negative circumstances, we will create a wall of negativity around us.

Prosperous people focus on creating success in the thing or things to which they are called. They are able to transcend the limitations of their heredity, environment, education, and their present circumstances. They have eyes to see what others cannot see.

Ultimately, prosperity is a state of mind. It is a mind-set developed by constant focus on what is good and right for your life. As stated in the book, *The Battle for the Mind,* "When battling opposing forces in the mind, you must understand that whoever or whatever controls your mind controls you.

You are essentially mind."[1] This is an important truth when it comes to developing a vow of prosperity for your life. The victory for prosperity is first won in your mind (your emotions and attitudes) and then secured by your actions.

Let's look at it this way. You are in financial chaos. Debt is mounting and out of control. What happens? You look at the pile of bills while looking at your bank account, and you start to go crazy. You look at how much you need and what you don't have, and the feelings of limitations and fear grip your heart. The more you focus on those negative feelings, the more the negative energies grow, magnetizing even more lack, more debt, less income. The only way to create a spirit of prosperity is to rise above the circumstances and believe that there is a higher way for you. Envision that way, and allow God to give you the strategy to reach what you see.

A Man Takes a Journey

Returning to Jesus' parable about the talents (Matt. 25:14-29), there are phrases that He uses that warrant a deeper look:

1. *"Going away on a trip"*—This is a good figure of speech for the interim time between the two advents. We live between two worlds, and His presence is not as manifest as it shall be when He returns. How shall we then live until the time when He returns?

2. *"Summonded his own servants"*—This statement reminds us to whom we belong. We are not our own, nor do we own our possessions. Servant—that is the nature of who we are, and is the foundation of all relationships—how we relate to God and to others.

3. *"And turned over his property to them"*—Notice that the servants are not treated like little children. They are given greater responsibilities and treated like adults. Giving is the outward manifestation of grace. God places certain abilities and commodities into our hands and then expects us to use those gifts for His purposes. Entrusting these gifts into their hands means a measure of faith in them. He entrusted them because he trusted them.

4. *"To one He gave five talents, and to another two, and to another one..."*—to each and every one (*hekasto,* Greek) according to one's unique ability. Our call to salvation is equal, but our gifts in the Kingdom of God are not equal. Our gifts and callings are apportioned by a wise Lord's knowledge of His servant's ability. No one is urged beyond His ability. "Each" plays an important role in the doctrine of gifts. Each of us is a unique *idian* or *idiosyncratic* and has been given a uniquely crafted gift.

The sums entrusted to the servants were graded by their capacity. The trust of the Lord to each servant is measured according to his mental ability, wealth, position, or influence.

"According to the ability of each one—according as he saw each one was adapted to improve it. So in the church and the world. God gives people stations which He judges them adapted to fill, and requires them to fill them. He makes distinctions among people in regard to abilities, and in the powers and opportunities of usefulness, requiring them only to occupy those stations, and to discharge their duties there."[2]

God has gifted you, and these divine enablings are given to you based on your capacity to improve the world around you with those gifts. He only requires that you stand in your place and not in another one's place.

ENDNOTES

1. Noel Jones, *The Battle for the Mind* (Destiny Image Publishers, Shippensburg, PA), 2006.

2. Barnes Notes on the New Testament, from Theophilos Digital Bookcase, © 1998, International Bible Translators.

CHAPTER THREE

Establishing Your Core Values

One of the first steps to prosperity is to determine what your core values are. Each of us has our own unique set of personal core values that guide our lives. Core values are our essential and enduring beliefs and guiding principles that motivate us and to which we give priority. They provide the structure to our lives.

The understanding and setting of core values is critical. In order to find your core values you have to penetrate who you pretend to be and think you are, in order to discover who you really are. In the psychology of perception, known as gestalt, the mind and the eye need to restore what is incomplete. That which you know and that which you perceive, influence how you view your world and impact how you interact with the world around you. The merging values of this interaction create the emerging core values that guide your life.

If we asked you what your core values are, most people would struggle to find the answer. You would not be alone; in fact the majority of people would find it hard to answer this question satisfactorily. You know what you do, but why do you do it? What inner motivation guides you through life?

In this chapter you will discover the principles of generational wealth creation that is founded on key core values. These truths are like a street fight. You must start with the basics, then apply them both aggressively and defensively—and never, ever quit.

You cannot be successful in life unless you understand what your core values are, have evaluated them, adjusted them if necessary, and then made a personal commitment to not change those values—no matter what.

There are an abundance of core values that people could commit to. Discussed here are the core values that have made us successful:

- Integrity.

- Discipline.

- Knowledge.

- Fellowship.

- Faith.

- Loyalty.

INTEGRITY

Integrity comprises the personal inner sense of "wholeness" deriving from honesty and consistent uprightness of character. Do what you say, do your best, remain at one with yourself, and be honest in all that you do with others. Integrity is the foundation upon which character is built. In her book, *The Energy of Money*, Maria Nemeth says that the Standards of Integrity are your reference points for personal power.[1]

Honesty, truthfulness, reliability, and honor should be the basis for the power and strength that emanate from your life.

The core requirements for the individual as well as those in top management include integrity, intelligence, and energy. It's been said that Warren Buffett, one of the world's wealthiest men, considers three qualities when hiring someone: integrity, intelligence, and energy—because if they don't have the first, the other two will kill you. This statement of truth is from the most successful investor in history, and Mr. Buffett is absolutely correct. Integrity must be in the soul of all that you do; and if it is, you and your efforts will be honored by God.

King David asked the Lord, "O Lord, who may abide in Thy tent? Who may dwell on Thy holy hill?[2] And then he answered his own question: "He who walks with integrity, and works righteousness, and speaks truth in his heart."[3]

Integrity is righteous! The Jewish prophet Isaiah said, "Say to the righteous that it will go well with them, for they will eat the fruit of their actions."[4] Integrity is at the heart of all human relationships and transactions. It is the foundation for forming lasting human relationships and it is at the core of all human interactions. Without it families will fail and corporations will fall. You cannot be successful and reach your goals until integrity has been fashioned into the very fabric of your being.

The sign of a person who is walking in the highest level of integrity is that the individual will always perform the highest quality of work in everything they do. People of integrity are always honest with themselves. They seek to do excellent work at every opportunity. The person who is defined by integrity understands that everything they do is a statement about who they are as a person.

You will inevitably attract into your life the type of people and circumstances that are in harmony with your dominant thoughts and values. If you cheat and lie then that is what you will attract into your life. But if you walk in the ways of integrity then, like a magnet, you will draw people of integrity into your life. It is not enough that you have established integrity in your life; you must surround yourself with people of integrity.

DISCIPLINE

Discipline is the bridge between goals and accomplishments. If discipline is not added to your vision there can be no success. Discipline is truly the bridge between the goals that you set and the fulfillment of those goals. George Washington said that discipline is the soul of an army. It makes small numbers formidable, procures success for the weak, and brings honor to all.

Discipline has to be manifested in every step of the journey—discipline in your time management, discipline in your finances, discipline in your work ethic, discipline in every area of your life. Discipline will guard you against the frivolous and other things that compete for your attention. You have to discipline yourself to do the things you need to do when you need to do them.

Harry Emerson Fosdick, a great theologian of the last century, had this to say about discipline: "No horse gets anywhere until he is harnessed. No stream or gas drives anything until it is confined. No Niagara is ever turned into light and power until it is tunneled. No life ever grows great until it is focused, dedicated, disciplined."[5]

Time management requires that you have a personal written schedule of events in order to control the chaos of demands upon your life. Here are some keys that will help you manage your time.

To Do List. Write down the things you have to do. Then decide what to do at the moment, what to schedule for later, what to get someone else to do, and what to put off for a later time.

Daily/Weekly Planner. Write appointments, classes, and meetings in a chronological log book or chart. If you are more visual, sketch out your schedule first thing in the morning. Check what's ahead for the day, and always go to sleep knowing you're prepared for tomorrow.

Long-term Planner. Use a monthly chart so you can plan ahead.

Time For Your Life. Perform the following exercise. View a typical month in terms of how you allocate your time. How much time do you spend at work, at home, with your mate, kids, family, or friends? Do your best to honestly chart all of your daily, weekly, and monthly activities into a "typical" month.

Analyze the results by first separating your activities into "personal" and "business" sectors. On the personal side, does your allocation of time comport with your belief system regarding your priorities? Are you in line with your core social, spiritual, and personal values?

When dissecting your working input, is the output satisfactory? If you have 75 percent of your wealth tied up in or derived from real estate investment that required 10 percent of your time to accumulate and/or manage, shouldn't you consider a potential shift in your labor input to control rather than be controlled by your output (or lack thereof)?

Financial discipline demands that you have a budget. Control your money. Do not let money control you. Discipline yourself to make sure that the flow of your money is gong in the right direction at all times.

For managing your finances, if you haven't started already, you should start an expense journal today. Begin with a manageable commitment. Write down every dollar you spend over the next 30 days. Categorize your expenditures in a thematic fashion, e.g., household expenses, leisure, business, and necessities.

If you can continue to track your spending thereafter, two certainties will transpire. First, you will spend less money than you would have absent the visibility tracking your expenses provides. Second, you will be developing the discipline necessary to accumulate true wealth. If, however, you can't last beyond the first 30 days, calculate to the best of your ability what you spent during the month you failed to meticulously chart your spending.

If you are honest with yourself, you will notice an increase in unnecessary spending when you "aren't watching." This same principal extends to employees and children. Nothing reaches its potential without attention; and constant attention requires discipline.

KNOWLEDGE

It's been said that an individual who is active in higher *learning* soon becomes an individual active in higher earning. Knowledge is power and must not be forfeited for a journey down side streets and alleys.

Learn everything you can. Read as much as you can on every subject related to your passion and calling. Before crossing over into Canaan, Joshua challenged the Jewish people with this words: "Do not let the Book of the Law depart from your mouth; meditate on it day and night, so that you may be careful to do everything written in it. Then you will be prosperous and successful" (Josh. 1:8). The Hebrew prophet Hosea declared that, "My people are destroyed for lack of knowledge..." (Hos. 4:6).

A book is a treasure that you can open again and again, and each time it will unfold new treasures. A man's treasure can be found in his bookcase. Albert Einstein said that information is not knowledge. It is not enough to simply collect information. You must take the information that you have collected and move it into knowledge and then the knowledge has to be transformed into wisdom.

Where does one obtain knowledge? Knowledge comes from a variety of sources: reading, life experiences, relationship with others, and revelation. Acquiring knowledge is one of the keys to success; for knowledge increases our mental capacity to fulfill our vision. Buying books related to your vision, talking to other people, your own personal experiences and revelation from God, are all ways that knowledge passes into our lives.

FELLOWSHIP

As mentioned, knowledge is also a means of acquiring fellowship. While study in whatever form comports with your circumstance, knowledge is also derived at a deep and critical level from fellowship. Seek the counsel of those more informed in the disciplines who will advance your goals. Many people, particularly those of strong will, character, and often times those in leadership roles, tend to surround themselves with people who "see it the way they do."

It is unfortunate that people who tell us how good and right we are make us feel good. If that were not the case, perhaps we would then seek counsel from those who tell us the truth. Wouldn't you prefer to know that you were not wearing any clothes?

In George S. Clason's classic work, *The Richest Man in Babylonian,* an intriguing dialogue ensued between Bansir, the chariot builder, and Kobbi, the musician. Their frustration over their perception of a lack of reward for their lives' hard work was reflected in their conversation as follows:

"Might we not find out how others acquire gold and do as they do?" Kobbi inquired.

"Perhaps there is some secret we might learn if we but sought those who knew it," replied Bansir thoughtfully.

Prosperity, if we are to attain it, must be sought, and through the application of core values we can attain it, especially the application of the core values of knowledge and fellowship. If you seek knowledge through fellowship, ultimately "each helps the other and says to his brother, 'be strong'" (Isa. 41:6 NIV).

The fellowship between the authors of this book afforded each significant insight and understanding into the culture and tools collected by the other; the result of which, beyond lifelong friendship, has expanded our respective circles to spheres of influence internationally and led to the creation and maintenance of wealth and prosperity for us, the Church and its members, at home, nationally and abroad.

We founded Urban Consulting upon the premise that together we can achieve greatness. Consequently, the aggregation of the best of the best in their respective business, legal, and financial disciplines created a confluence of talent designed to foster quantum advances in our clients' evolution and the achievement of their respective goals.

One client, Homer T. Hayward Lumber Company, once it embraced this premise, achieved 500 percent growth in 10 years. Now Hayward Lumber's Mission Statement reads: "We believe the right people, given the right resources and freedom, can achieve greatness." Bishop Jones' church, City of Refuge in Gardena, California, having adopted the same premise, has grown over 1,000 percent during the same period of time.

FAITH

All things are from God, and absent faith, the sheep remain wandering in the wilderness. "Then the Lord your God will make you most prosperous in all the work of your hands and in the fruit of your womb, the young of your livestock and the crops of your land. The Lord will again delight in you and make you prosperous..." (Deut. 30:9 NIV).

As you embark upon your journey, many of the turns in the road of your life are and will continue to be, at present, unknown to you. Your success will come if you have faith, both in yourself and in God and although, "your beginnings will seem humble, so prosperous will your future be" (Job 8:7).

Your faith will allow you to persevere through hard times, flourish during good times, and stay the course regardless of the doubts and criticisms others of lesser conviction will undoubtedly hurl at you. The greater the opposition others demonstrate regarding your decisions and the faith you place in them, the greater likelihood exists in terms of their appropriateness and the results they will deliver. Never, ever stop fighting for what you believe in. Have faith!

LOYALTY

Loyalty, like respect, is an earned state of being. It inures not only people but to ideals, beliefs, values, and God. Your core value of faith is a demonstration of your loyalty to God.

In the Old Testament, on Yom Kippur, people were (and remain today) required to first seek and obtain forgiveness from one another before seeking God's forgiveness. Loyalty is a divine principal, particularly loyalty to one another and God. An absence of loyalty is an infectious character flaw that will impair and prevent your prosperity if it enters your life.

Take care of those who are loyal to you. This does not mean you promote people to positions that transcend their skill sets because they are loyal, for ultimately, doing so would promote a loyal person's failure through no fault of their own. It does, however, mean that a loyalist is deserving of, as Jim Collins says in his best-selling book *Good to Great*, the right seat on the bus.[6] Everyone you attract into your life, the loyalist included, has an appropriate seat on the bus if and when you decide to travel the path toward your prosperity. Loyalty is a necessarily reciprocal trait which starts with you.

ENDNOTES

1. Maria Nemeth, *The Energy of Money* (New York: Ballantine Wellspring, 1997), 59.

2. Ps. 15:1.

3. Ps. 15:2.

4. Isa. 3:10.

5. http://www.quoteworld.org/quotes/4872.

6. Jim Collins, *Good to Great and the Social Sectors* (New York: HarperCollins, 2005).

CHAPTER FOUR

Personal Economics 101

Wealth should never be the goal. Most people who try to achieve it use what others have accumulated as the measuring sticks for their own success. First, without a deep understanding of the facts and circumstances behind others' success, comparing their experiences to your own will produce an inapposite result that provides you no tangible benefit.

The race and the victory remain with you. In order to win the financial and success race you have to start with the basics. You have to deal with the nature of who you are and the environment in which you presently exist.

Every one of us has to deal with heredity and environment. For most of us these are the obstacles we have to recognize and overcome. By using heredity effectively you can modify your environment. To the extent that you exploit your abilities, you will be prosperous.

Goethe, a prolific German writer in the 18th century, wrote that debt is a tool of the devil. The first rule of personal economics is to overcome the debt issues in your life. Do not succumb to the marketing media that pushes you to buy what you do not need using funds you do not have.

The basic tools in society involve communication. Even if you have limited abilities in English and math, it is worth investing in increasing your skills in communication and math. These are the tools of the game. They are the tools of succeeding in life. Take advantage of the schooling that is available to you. As your life progresses and society changes, developing an ability to adapt by exploring and exploiting new skills will bring a new force into your personal economics.

A life of learning, exploring, and exploiting ever new abilities, besides providing a sound basis for personal economics, can be a personally satisfying and rewarding life, much more satisfying than being a slave to others.

Here are some basic keys to developing your own personal economics.

LIFE SKILLS AND THE RIGHT JOB

There are too many people who feel locked in the wrong job. They hate getting up in the morning and heading off to work. They find no joy in their work. Here is the good news. You don't have to stay in that dungeon. There are keys to finding the right job for you. The first step is to identify what you want to do and what you can do successfully. When you find your path, traveling it will no longer be considered "work."

This will take some effort on your part. You will have to search your soul to find the answer to what you want to do and what can you do successfully. Here is one exercise to help you. If you had all the money you needed to do what you wanted, what would you do? After you have answered that question, then answer the second part. Do you have the skills, education, and experience to do what you want? If not, do you have the core values to get it?

Even if the answer is "no," don't stop at this point. Find a way to develop your skills, educate yourself, and get the experience you need. If the goal is worth it, then the struggle to attain that goal will be worth your effort. You will have to learn how to market yourself. Overcome anxiety and fear. Know that God has created you with design and purpose and has gifted you with skills and abilities to reach the destiny He has put in your soul.

Personal Budgeting

We will have more to say about budgets in the following chapter, but there are some introductory comments here. When you have reached your career goal you have only solved one problem. One of the laws of economics is "supply and demand." You have resolved the supply side. You are creating finances that are able to meet the demands of your lifestyle.

But you must learn how to effectively budget those resources or the resources that you have created will not meet the demands of your life. The students in our seminars work in small groups and use hypothetical information to develop a personal budget for a teenager. They learn the reasons for creating a budget and the basic features and characteristics of all budgets.

Do you know how to balance your checkbook? If not, your local bank will often help you learn how or you can take a personal finance course which may be free of charge at a community center or local community college. How much did you spend on entertainment last year? Food? Rent? Can you trim expenses? How much would one less daily dessert Latte save you per year? Do the math.

Do you have the skills, education, and experience to do the job you want to do? Though the visceral response of most people is an unequivocal "no," are you really sure that answer is correct? In truth, the talents parable isn't saying, "nothing ventured, nothing gained," but rather "nothing *measured*, nothing gained."

As discussed in the chapter on budgeting, after our life vision and the articulation, in writing, of our goals, we need to measure what we spend and categorize it to form an understanding of our spending habits (this, of course, applies in business as well as personal finances). We can't change what we don't understand, and once we understand the patterns of our spending, we can formulate a game plan about how to affect those patterns. Change, like saving and investing money, requires discipline. Start by balancing your checkbook, categorizing all of your monthly expenses, and making a budget.

A budget is a plan for managing your finances and is necessary for financial freedom. The main objective for any budget is to gain visibility and control over your money to prevent a lack of money controlling you. By predicting and accommodating future expenses and sacrificing nonmandatory spending in favor of necessary spending or a savings goal, you can achieve your personal financial goals.

The more complicated the budgeting process is, the less likely a person is to maintain it. The purpose of a personal budget is to identify where income and expenditure is present in the common household; it is not to identify each individual purchase ahead of time.

USING CREDIT WISELY

Be careful of the credit card trap. Credit cards can be wonderful tools for managing your financial resources and establishing credit, but you need to make sure you manage them correctly. Using credit cards can help you build a positive credit history. This can enhance your ability to receive a private student loan, buy a car, rent an apartment, get a job, start a business and eventually, buy a house or investment property. Of course, there are other advantages to having a credit card including: security in legitimate emergencies, reducing the need to carry cash, and the ability to track expenses through the review of detailed statements.

You will need to be very careful in the cards you choose. Look closely at the interest rates. Here are some tips on managing your credit cards:

1. Watch for carrying balances month to month. Some cards charge 20 percent or more in interest. (Interest is usually called "finance charges" on your billing statements and cause you to pay more in the long-term for that item that was "on sale.")

2. Fixed rates aren't always fixed! A credit card company can increase the rate by informing you 15 days before changing the rate.

3. Look at your monthly billing statement carefully and call the company right away if you have any questions.

4. There is usually a large finance charge for cash advances and interest begins accruing as soon as you take the money out, not after the next statement closing.

5. Be aware of annual fees. Many times you are charged $50 or more just to have the card.

6. Watch out for introductory offers! When you receive a credit card offer in the mail with a low rate, it may

expire in three or six months. Note when and by how much the rate increases after the "introductory offer" expires. You may not remember when it expires, but the card company will!

7. Think about your purchases. If you are not able to afford the purchase now, chances are you won't be able to afford it in a month when the credit card bill arrives!

8. If you dispute an item, do so in writing, and keep records of your expenses, statements, and correspondence for five years.

CHAPTER FIVE

Making a Paradigm Shift

In 1962, Thomas Kuhn wrote The Structure of Scientific Revolution, and fathered, defined, and popularized the concept of "paradigm shift." Kuhn argued that scientific advancement is not evolutionary, but rather is a "series of peaceful interludes punctuated by intellectually violent revolutions," and in those revolutions "one conceptual world view is replaced by another."[1]

He encouraged us to think of a paradigm shift as a change from one way of thinking to another. It's a revolution, a transformation—a sort of metamorphosis. It doesn't just happen, but rather "agents of change" must activate the reformation.

A change from one way of thinking to another—in order to *act* differently you must first *think* differently. One of the great keys to financial freedom is learning to think differently. For most of you this will take a paradigm shift that takes you out of the old mind-sets of insecurity, poverty mentality, and fear of failure. You cannot go forward until you break free from the thoughts of the past that bind you and keep you from moving ahead. You have to get out of the box created by negative concepts that have been pounded into your psyche by adverse circumstances throughout your life. Dispute certain popular beliefs, poverty is not divine. Do you find it interesting that those who preach the poverty mentality are rarely poor? Beware of false prophets as you make your vow of prosperity.

Most of us don't even realize that we are trapped in a paradigm, but our conversations and actions often betray us. It is God's desire to strip you of the paradigms that betray you, and set you free so you can think in a brand-new way and see life from His perspective.

THINKING CORRECTLY

Soren Kierkegaard, the Danish theologian, said that people demand freedom of speech as a compensation for the freedom of thought which they seldom use. If we are going to make a vow of prosperity, we must be able to articulate what we have thought through. Thought is connected to wealth. It is the stream that leads to the wealth we all seek.

Man is unique among all God's creation in that he has the power of thought. He has a mind that can reason, imagine, emote, and perceive. The mind refers to the collective aspects of the intellect and consciousness that are a combination of thought, perception, emotion, memory, will, and imagination. If you are going to become a prosperous person, you will have to learn how to control and exercise your mind.

You must control the direction of the mind that tends to drift into negativity and the mundane. These thought patterns would prevent you from reaching your goals and fulfilling your destiny. You must also learn how to exercise your mind, developing it through reading and talking with others about subjects that will challenge your thinking processes. Remember the core value of fellowship, and reach for those who teach.

Improve Your Thinking

The biggest roadblock to success can be your *thinking*. In order to increase your mental capacity, you must pay attention to what you are thinking. The following series of questions for you to answer will help determine the direction and focus of your thoughts.

- What do you spend your time focusing on?

- Are your thoughts positive or negative?

- Do you think complaining thoughts...or uplifting thoughts?

- Are you grateful for all you have...or focused on lack?

- Do you recognize your successes?

- How often do you look down, rather than up the ladder?

- Do you look for learning opportunities?

- Does fear dominate your mind?

- Do you doubt yourself or your worth?

- Do you see the difficulties and inconveniences...or blessings?

- Can you see the future...your dreams? Do you believe they can be your reality?

- Do you view situations objectively and respond...or react in the midst of them?

- Do you buy into negative self-talk or negative thoughts about others?

Your Mind Affects Your Speech and Your Actions

The Bible says, "...out of the abundance of the heart, the mouth speaks" (Matt. 12:34). The mouth is the expression of your thoughts. What you are thinking is expressed in what you say and do. The mouth is the external manifestation of one's character and disposition.

The chief way that God has designed us to express ourselves is through speech. If you change your thinking, you will change your speaking. If you change your speaking, then you can reset your future. A changed or renewed mind will reset the life that is before you.

The thoughts of the mind are usually expressed through the words of the mouth and our actions or inactions. You can determine the intelligence of a person by what they say and do (and sometimes by what they refrain from saying or doing). Thinking people are expressive people—philosophically, artistically, and spiritually. The more powerful your thoughts, the greater the possibilities that exist for you.

You were created with a mind capable of great thought. The comparable sin is that so few use their mind to its fullest extent (or even close).

The Mind of the Maker

Dorothy Sayers, in her book *The Mind of the Maker*, draws an intriguing analogy between the Trinity and the development of a book. Every book, she says, begins in the mind of its creator. The setting, personalities, and the story line are creations formed in the thoughts of the writer. Those thoughts are eventually transformed into words forming the content of a book eventually to be read by the reader.[2]

In the shadows of eternity, an awesome idea for a wonderful story was being developed. Before there was time, before there was space, when all was God, a brilliant plot was wrapping itself around a grace-full idea. These passionate ideas and plans were being formed in the mind of the Creator and cast a shadow over all His beloved creation: *the shadow of His presence.*

The imaginations creating the story were in harmony with the love flowing out of Father's heart. Stimulating the thinking in His mind were the powerful passions stirring in His heart. The thoughts in His mind were eventually translated into words—words that would form the outline of an incredible plan.

In the beginning, the Scriptures tell us, was the Word. The Word was the full expression of the thoughts of this magnificent Maker. But before a word could exist, there must be thoughts, conceived from an inspired idea.

Divine deliberations, timeless thoughts, creative concepts, powerful plans were assembling themselves into an amazing arrangement of literary genius. The ideas stretching forth from His mind longed for their moment of unveiling.

So it is with all of us. Before you can express dynamic words and exhibit success in your life, you will have to think with the mind given to you by your Maker. There are thoughts and ideas that God has given you that are waiting to be birthed.

By reorienting your thinking you have been changed from within. If you commit yourself to this process you will be successful and fulfill your vow of prosperity.

CHANGED FROM THE INSIDE

"But be ye transformed by the renewing of your mind...." These are the words that apostle Paul wrote to the church in Rome in the first century. (See Romans 12:2.) He understood that outward transformation was dependent on an inner renewing of the mind. If you are going to change all of the negative habits regarding your life then you must begin inside your head, in your thinking. You will never be successful if you don't *think* you can be successful. You will never generate new ideas if you think that you are dumb or unworthy. Success is a matter of the mind that has been changed by God.

We live in a time that will require new thoughts and fresh ideas. Abraham Lincoln said that the dogmas of the quiet past are inadequate for the stormy present. The occasion is piled high with difficulty, and we must rise with the occasion. As our case is new, so we must think anew and act anew.[3]

We need to change our thinking and our actions. Henry Drummond, perhaps best-remembered as a gifted evangelist who assisted Dwight L. Moody during his revival campaigns, was also a lecturer in natural science. In his lectures, he discussed the three laws of natural science and their influence in changing man. The three laws are: the law of *motion*, the law of *assimilation*, and the law of *influence*.

The law of assimilation states that we hold in permanent preservation the things that we reflect. By what power do we retain those things upon which we reflect? In computer and accounting lingo we say, *garbage in, garbage out*. Input into a computer is retained in its memory banks for immediate access. Whatever you put into your mind will be reflected in your actions. Therefore, as apostle Paul stated, it is best to reflect on all that is good and pure and holy. (See Philippians 4:8.)

The law of influence declares that we become like those whom we habitually admire. People are mosaics of other people. No man is an island. No one exists in this life in a vacuum. Therefore we are the result of the influence or impact other people have had on our lives—for good or for evil. Your thought life will be impacted by the words of others. As established in the chapter on core values, fellowship is a core value. The kind of people you hang out with will influence your thoughts and determine your ability to change.

ENDNOTES

1. Thomas Kuhn, *The Structure of Scientific Revolutions* (University of Chicago, 1962).

2. Dorothy Sayers, *The Mind of the Maker* (New York: Continuum International Publishing Group, 2004).

3. http://www.wisdomquotes.com/cat_changegrowth.html.

CHAPTER SIX

Managing Your Money

THE TALENT

The talent (*kikkar*) was the largest unit of weight in the Bible. The relation between the talent and the shekel is defined in Exodus 38:25-26. The half shekel brought by 603,550 men amounted to 100 talents and 1,775 shekels. Thus a talent was 3,000 shekels.[1]

A talent was equal to 10,000 Greek denari. A denari, we learn in the Parable of the Workers in the Vineyard, is a fair day's wage. Ten thousand denari is a lifetime of wages. The least talented servant had a life of wages. God gives gifts to you that will sustain you for a lifetime. Grace gives you the power for a lifetime. Talent for a lifetime—gifted for a lifetime—not temporarily but permanently.

You are gifted to repossess, to take back all that was yours. Gifted to start again. Gifted to continue as the Lord directs. It is time to make your vow of prosperity in all that you do.

MANAGING THE PROCESS

The process of managing your gifts to be successful has a beginning in terms of your finances and your life. Everything must be budgeted, including your time. The budget is the fundamental underpinning; and if approached with discipline and consistency, will provide you the visibility necessary to control your life rather than having your life control you.

How can you achieve a goal you don't set? What if you fail to budget enough time to achieve the goals you do set? Take control—start right now.

THE PERSONAL BUDGET

Every enterprise, including your family, has multiple income and expense items that can and must be budgeted if success (however defined) is a goal. If your goal is to move from your apartment to your first home, some elementary questions must be asked and answered. Can you guess what they are? Here are some examples:

When would you like to own your own home or investment property?

How much can you afford to spend?

How much does the type of property you want cost?

How much money do you currently earn?

What do you presently spend?

Can you decrease your expenses, increase your income, and save enough for a down payment?

If yes, will you be able to afford servicing the debt?

Without time and financial budgets in place, a review of these questions will reveal that you will probably stay in the apartment where you are currently living—or worse, have to return to the apartment because you couldn't make your home mortgage payments.

These principles transcend home ownership and permeate every successful business enterprise globally from Microsoft to your church.

Let's extrapolate from the home acquisition example and assume that you are single with two young children. Your budget would begin with a time goal. You decide that in two years you *will be* (not you will *try* to be) in your own home. The size of your family will dictate, in large measure, the number of bedrooms and thus the price (area and amenities depending) of your target.

Having set the initial time budget, we move on to the income side of your budget. Again, we start from the beginning. What is your monthly income? Write that number on a piece of paper. Bisect the page so the income number is in the left column. Now, one line beneath the income figure, let's begin enumerating your expenses one by one. Leave nothing out. It is better to err on the side of conservative income numbers and aggressive expense numbers.

We need an accurate, real-time picture of where you are so we can help modify it toward where you want to, and will, be. Include your monthly expenses: rent, automobile payment, gas, insurance, food, clothes, telephone, cable, entertainment, religious and/or charitable contributions, and anything else you can think of. Now subtract the total of your monthly expenses from the total amount of your monthly income.

Many people are shocked to find out that they actually have a negative number. Don't be concerned. You bought this book to help you achieve your goals, one of which was and remains massive change toward prosperity and the creation of generational wealth. That type of change takes many people decades to accomplish. Properly executed, however, it will happen much faster for you.

Now we need to determine what exactly you are budgeting for, that is short-, middle-, and long-term goals. For the purposes of this text, we will stick with the homeownership example. Since this hypothetical assumes that your children are young, budgeting for college, weddings, and the like are not relevant at this time. Together, your budget and goals form the beginnings of your life plan.

EXPENSE REDUCTION

Start with your largest recurring expenses. Any room? Don't get discouraged at this point. This is the hard part— harder than acquiring property, believe it or not. Buckle down.

Do you have more than one credit card?

Have you compared the interest rates?

Can you transfer balances to lower interest rate cards?

Can you redirect some of your expenditures toward retiring high interest debt?

Can you eat out less?

Start with the down payment figure you would need to acquire the property you want and work backward. If your goal is to own a new home within two years, how much a month must you save over the next 24 months to amass that sum? Does it now appear more feasible?

Don't worry, at this juncture, about whether or not it appears easy. We still have arrows in our quiver. Also remember that, unlike rent, interest paid on a primary residence is deductible. As such, the taxes you pay will be reduced, thus reducing your expenses. This remains true even if your mortgage and your rent are equal, and even if some of the money you need to complete the purchase is represented by funds borrowed from the seller.

SAVE AND BE SAVED

Some people claim to spend their time working. Others invest their time learning. The principles regarding time can be extended to money. Remember the holistic approach to prosperity involving your mind, spirit, and body.

If you refrained from ordering dessert for a month and saved that money, you could start accumulating a nest egg. Are there any other aspects of your existence that could be trimmed to afford you the ability to accumulate a small investment pool? Look at your budget. What would a mere 10 percent reduction in your annual expenses yield? Over two years, could you assemble enough capital to make a small investment? Probably so. Remember, prosperity is a choice. You could choose to borrow money from a rich relative to pay your past due rent, accumulate more debt, and dig a deeper hole; or the same relative could become an equity partner in a duplex you buy and collect money from. What choice will you make?

Ultimately, prosperity is the product of hard choices and even harder work. Some people would rather have the extra slice of cake and the second car. Most people are not prosperous. Are you ready to make the hard choices? Reduce your variable expenses (those that are not fixed, recurring expenses such as rent) by 10 percent for one month. If you are miserable, order the extra slice of cake. If you are not, welcome to the road to prosperity! Keep up the good, hard work, and enjoy the ride. Decide to ride with God on your side. Save and be saved.

ENDNOTE

1. http://www.jewishvirtuallibrary.org/jsource/History/weightsandmeasures.html.

CHAPTER SEVEN

Avoiding the Money Pit

One of the great keys to avoiding the money pit is to empower yourself to get to the next level of greatness. The Scriptures say that the wealth of the wicked is laid up for the just (see Ecclesiastes 2:26); but how do we go about accessing it?

In order to access wealth, we must position ourselves in a place to secure and sustain that wealth. Good personal credit and excellent business credit are two of the vehicles that will help you get there. Without good credit, you will not be able to function in the world of finances. Credit allows access and leverage, and both inure to the benefit of wealth creation.

GOOD CREDIT, STRONG CORE FOUNDATIONS, AND FINANCING

It takes money to make money. Though true, the money "it takes" does not need to be yours. Without good credit you will not be able buy a house, purchase a car, invest in a business, or do many of the other things that you have established as goals in your life. Establishing good credit is a seminal task toward moving in the direction of financial freedom.

First, you have to know what your credit score is. Your credit score helps you determine where you are and where you need to go. A credit score is a number generated by a mathematical algorithm—a formula—based on information in your credit profile report, compared to information relating to tens of millions of other people. The resulting number is a prediction of how likely you are to pay your bills. Low credit scores can bind you and keep you in financial servitude.

Second, you need to know what is in your credit report, whether it's accurate or if you have been a victim of identity theft. Until you know exactly what your credit report reveals about you and your credit history, you will never be able to investigate any possible inaccuracies or fraudulent activity that may have occurred. Your credit report will help you identify as well as quantify and qualify your debt.

There are many Websites that will help you obtain a free credit report. Get your report and start working on establishing a better credit score. A good score is necessary to buying (and affording) a car, getting a mortgage, and many other necessities of life.

Your FICO Score

A FICO score is a generic credit score developed by Fair, Isaac and Company, Inc., that was designed to predict the possibility of borrowers becoming seriously delinquent in their credit obligations. Your FICO score is comprised of five distinct areas:

1. 35% – Payment history.

2. 30% – Amounts owed.

3. 15% – Types of credit.

4. 10% – New credit.

5. 10% – Length of credit history.

The higher your FICO score, the less you pay to buy on credit. The lower your cost of borrowed funds, the more resources you have left over to invest and achieve prosperity. A credit score, used by the vast majority of lenders to approve or deny the granting of credit, is defined largely as a statistical analysis of a consumers' creditworthiness generated, in part, from information on a credit report. A credit report tracks credit consumers' payment records on individual credit accounts and reveals how well or how poorly each account is managed by the consumer.

The system uses a numerical score but also a letter grading system, scoring consumers from A to F.

901-990 = A

801-900 = B

701-800 = C

601-700 = D

501-600 = F

The dominant FICO score ranges from 350 to 850 with no letter grading system. Generally, the higher the score the more likely you are to qualify for a home loan and the lower the interest rate and better the terms.

The three main credit bureaus, Equifax, Experian Information Systems, and TransUnion collectively receive, maintain, and publish information reported to them by your creditors. You can obtain copies of your credit score for free by contacting Experian at http://www.dmv.org/free-credit-report.php.

Creditors look at your combined or median score when determining whether you are an acceptable credit risk and at what price credit should be extended to you. Again, start from a position of strength which is synonymous with knowledge. Understand how the credit rating process works, how you can affect it, and what to do first, second, and third, etc. when building or rebuilding your credit profile.

What Makes Up Your Credit Score?

Your credit score is an amalgamation of information relating to open credit, your payment history, the amount of your consumer debt, adverse claims reported by creditors, municipal and federal liens, including tax liens, court records and actions taken by and/or against you. The confluence of these elements is applied against a formula to result in a score recognized by creditors as an appropriate index against which to judge your credit worthiness.

Each of the three bureaus has a particular score, and most creditors seek either your median score or a particular bureau's score. Your FICO score is actually made up of the five actions/items listed previously. Certain actions taken by or against you, including the filing of a bankruptcy, the repossession of a car, or allowing a credit card issuer to charge off a debt, will have more severe ramifications in terms of your score than others such as being 30 days late paying credit cards or a car loan.

Learning how certain actions or inactions affect your credit can help you build your profile; and if, as often happens for many people, you fall behind and damage your profile, knowledge in terms of the mechanics of repairing your credit will direct you to take actions with your limited resources that will have the most dramatic effect regarding a point increase.

If you knew that your $500 properly applied would cause a 300-point increase if you paid one debt and a 50-point increase if you paid another, what would you do? Since your score has a linear bearing on how much creditors charge you, the result could be a higher interest rate which costs you tens of thousands of dollars over the life of a loan.

Why suffer this result because you chose not to seek counsel from someone with superior knowledge? After all, it was God who "appointed...those able to help others, those with gifts of administration..." (1 Cor. 12:28). God wants you to enjoy the benefits of fellowship and learn from those in whom He has vested gifts and talents.

COMMON MYTHS REGARDING CREDIT

Kimberly Washington, an expert credit counselor and manager of Urban's affiliate, Full Faith and Credit™, enumerates and demonstrates during Urban Seminars' Spiritual Solutions For Financial Freedom™ services, the *Top Ten Credit Myths*:

1. "When you pay off a past due account, such as a charge-off or a collection account, it will show 'paid,' and it will no longer be negative." Many actions affecting your credit score can be effectively managed. Inquiries, by way of example, even for the purpose of extending additional credit, adversely affect your score. Paying your bills late will, regardless of whether they are ultimately paid, show up as a derogatory reference. Charge-offs (paying the creditor less than they are owed and allowing the creditor to reflect just that on your credit report) is much worse. Neither, however, is necessary,

regardless of whether you are having tough times. If you are tight on money, *call your creditors* **before** *your bills are due.* Cut a deal up front, and confirm with your creditor that you expect him to refrain from reporting anything negative if you adhere to the agreement. Confirm that arrangement in writing. Extend that logic to the scenario where you must, for whatever reason, negotiate an arrangement with a creditor to resolve a debt for less than you owe. Confirm, in writing, before you pay the reduced sum, that no charge-off will be reported against you.

2. "If you succeed in deleting a negative item, it will simply come back on your credit report." This is not true, and if, for whatever reason, it does, you have the right to dispute, successfully, its presence. Remember, an improper derogatory reference on your credit report is slanderous, and the creditor or the credit bureau may be exposed to civil liability or worse. Document everything; keep good records. Remember, we are not victims. Don't act like one.

3. "There are negative items, such as bankruptcy and foreclosure, that are impossible to remove from your credit report." Nothing is impossible to have removed from your credit report. Some items last longer than others, but everyone is entitled to forgiveness; and all derogatory references will ultimately be removed from your report. Others never have to be there in the first place if you use the tools we are providing you.

4. "Disputing your credit report is easy, and anyone can do it for the price of a few postage stamps." Remember the principal of fellowship, and be efficient with your time. Hire an expert to assist you while you focus on the actions that are within your core skill sets. Leverage your time like you leverage your assets to maximize the return on the time invested, and

remember to invest rather than spend your time. Time is your most precious asset beyond your family, friends, and faith.

5. "If you declare bankruptcy, you can renew your credit like it never happened." You hear and read this myth advertised often. Certain types of bankruptcy can wipe out your debts, but nothing in federal bankruptcy law requires creditors to rescind negative remarks on your credit report following the filing, involuntarily or otherwise, of a bankruptcy. Forming a corporation or other entity and creating a new taxpayer identification number will likewise not eliminate the problems associated with a bankruptcy filing. Most creditors or potential creditors still require the social security number of the principal officer, director and/or shareholder, and when they run your credit, your bankruptcy will appear until removed from your personal credit profile.

6. "If you are not satisfied with the results of your credit bureau challenge, you may file a 100-word statement with the bureaus citing your side, and creditors will take your position into account." It is true that you can write 100 words on your credit report with your most eloquent prose, edifying the world about the severe injustice you suffered at the hands of the unfair creditor. That said, please remember that the entire credit reporting system is run by creditors who, together, designed and formed the system they feed to inform one another about good and bad credit risks as they see them. Your treatise will be, from their perspective, suspect and irrelevant. Save your eloquence for the conversation you are going to have with your creditors before derogatory references are reported against you.

7. "By changing numbers in your social security number or through the use of an employer's identification number,

you can fool credit bureaus into creating a clean, new credit profile for you." You could also rob a bank, and temporarily, if you do it just right, your money problems will be cured. That, like the foregoing myth, is a very, very bad idea. Attempting to defraud the federal government is a felony, and the penalties are far worse than the temporary burden of poor credit. Do it right. Seek the help and fellowship of professionals, and take your credit back.

8. "Enough good credit will obfuscate your bad credit." If only the dollar you saved paid off the ten you owed. Good credit is good. Get more of it. That said, we need to address and correct your bad credit, and endless good credit will not cure or even affect the bad.

9. "If you are having difficulty financially, a credit consolidator will be of benefit to you." Credit consolidators are agencies hired by consumers to distribute money to creditors in sums or increments less than the creditors are owed. This, from the perspective of institutional creditors, is the kiss of death, similar to a bankruptcy or a charge-off. Often the consolidator will, in addition to impugning your credit reputation by their very existence, allow, through their efforts, charge-offs as well. Just say no!

10. "It is illegal for a creditor to remove an accurate derogatory reference on your credit report." Creditors can do whatever they want with the derogatory references they place on your credit report. They may likewise refrain from placing them if you are proactive and can convince them to do so.

Tools

Multiple tools exist to assist you in the development of an appropriate credit profile. If you are a business, Dun &

Bradstreet, provider of international and U.S. business credit information and credit reports, will allow you to create a credit profile which those who extend credit to businesses will rely upon in determining your credit worthiness. While this type of tool is not presently available for individuals, most business organizations, including churches, are aware of this tool but don't know how to use it. Again, seek the advice of those who can easily help you navigate the process.

While the foregoing was limited in scope to personal credit, business credit will be addressed in detail in an upcoming chapter.

INVESTING

Once you exercise the discipline necessary to track your finances, curb consumer spending, budget, and improve your credit, you are ready to begin investing. Start with the premise that the amount of money you invest at first is far less significant than the fact that you are actually *investing*, rather than *spending* your money. Your nest egg will grow if you have integrity, discipline, knowledge, fellowship, loyalty, and faith.

This section of the book reviews several investment classes including equities and debt instruments, real estate, insurance-related products, and private equity investments. Also discussed are principles associated with each investment class. Each of these investment classes will be elaborated upon in substantial detail in future books, but for now, we will simply introduce you to the rhythm of investing and the truism that, regardless of your present belief system regarding your perceived economic obstacles, you can and will obtain prosperity if you so desire. Likewise, don't fear negative economic news or use it as an excuse for your failure to accumulate wealth. Fortunes are made in bad economic times.

We also cover the concept of appropriate *diversification.*

Finally, we explore and define the best investment you can ever make—an investment in yourself. Remember, investing is governed by the equation of risk versus reward. The premise being the greater the risk, the greater your expectation of the reward. Can you conceive of a less risky, better reward-laden investment than you? Once you recognize your potential to achieve anything and everything, invest everything you have in the best bet you can ever place.

How Much Is Too Much Debt?

We monitor our debt to equity (the value of a business or property beyond any mortgage or liability) ratio, debt coverage ratio, cash flow, and other salient financial indicators very closely. So do our lenders and investors. Whether you are managing your family's resources to ensure the ability to send your children to college, pay your rent, or acquire investment property, you must remain cognizant of how much leverage the structure you create can bear.

Your balance sheet (a statement reflecting your assets, liabilities and the difference, i.e., your net worth or lack thereof) will offer little more than bragging rights and a false sense of security if you can't pay your bills. Many, many people who were rich on paper in 1929, 1978, 1992, and other times throughout history, went bankrupt because they could not meet their obligations when they became due, a legal definition of insolvency since "the borrower is servant to the lender," (Prov. 22:7). We manage and reduce our debt at every conceivable turn.

Does your home cost more than 30 percent of your gross income? Do you stay awake at night worrying about your bills? Are you applying for new credit cards so you can continue to buy what you *need*?

You know when you have too much debt. That said, too much debt is not a permanent state of being for those willing to invest in themselves and change their circumstances. First, pay down your highest interest debt with whatever available resources you have. Then, budget debt reduction along with saving and investing.

Have a plan to become debt free, and work that plan. Write it down. Review your progress monthly, and commit to do better this month than you did the month before.

CHAPTER EIGHT

Planning for Your Future

INVESTMENTS

Many of you firmly believe that investments are for the rich, others with cash beyond your present circumstance. Wrong! Properly advised, anyone can invest and acquire wealth. This chapter explores equities, debt, real estate, and private equity investments you are capable of participating in. Many of the tools you require in order to start and grow your portfolio will be introduced to you. Let's get started.

EQUITIES AND DEBT

People and companies invest in equities and debt every day. For clarity, we will address equities first. Simply stated, equities are stock, and the most recognized form of stock investment is publicly traded common stock. You may participate at work in a 401(K) retirement plan which is an employer-sponsored qualified retirement savings plan. It allows you to save for your retirement while deferring any immediate income taxes on the money you save or their respective earnings until withdrawn. Your 401(K) may invest in mutual funds, a pooling arrangement designed to allow individual investors to acquire multiple stocks without having to invest the amount of money ordinarily required to do so. You may even track and/or own shares of common stock in a particular company or companies you believe will provide you a better return than a savings account or other alternative investment (the reward of a savings account is fairly low since the risk of losing a federally insured deposit is likewise fairly low).

Common Stock

The fundamentals of common stock, though they can vary, are typically as follows: 1) One vote per share; and 2) reward is measured by the appreciation in the stock price, and sometimes, by the dividend, i.e., a distribution of retained earnings (earnings less expenses).

Benefits of this type of investment include easy transferability if the equities are publicly traded on an exchange (The New York Stock Exchange, The Pacific Stock Exchange, NASDAQ, The Tokyo Stock Exchange, etc). Burdens include the ability to lose your entire investment; and further, in the event of closely held companies (those not publicly traded which, at present, account for the substantial majority of all companies in the United States) the difficulty associated with the sale and/or transfer of your equity interest. You may very well get trapped. Specifically, investments in debt have a higher priority upon liquidation than equity investments, and publicly traded equities are far more fungible than privately held equities.

Preferred Stock

Not all equities are entitled to one vote per share; and often, investors purchase preferred stock and trade their votes for additional security since this type of equity instrument is typically entitled to a preference upon a liquidation and a dividend preference. Consequently, preferred stock, as you will learn in the next section, is similar in character to debt from an investment perspective.

Closely Held Companies

Investments in closely held (non-public) corporations are referred to in this text as private equity investments. These come in many forms and sizes, many of which are beyond the scope of this text. We will focus on two distinct opportunities, namely forming and investing in your own business and investing, for endowment purposes or otherwise, in the businesses of others.

INVESTING IN YOURSELF

Forty percent of those employed by others are working on their own business interests on the side, be it trading on eBay or otherwise. Most are doing so either as sole proprietors or in a partnership consisting of one or more partners (whether they know it or not since partnerships can be formed de facto, by conduct). Neither of these scenarios offers any protection to you from liability which does or will exist while conducting business. In the partnership context, you are, in fact, jointly and severally liable for the actions and inactions of your partner. Further, neither form will assist you in obtaining outside capital since there are no shares to sell. For those reasons (and others), an entity should be formed when you decide to conduct business for yourself (including when you decide to acquire investment property). The type of entity will depend upon the type of business you intend to conduct, tax consequences, the number and character of co-owners, and multiple other considerations.

PRIVATE EQUITY

Investing in closely held corporations (or other similar entities) can be extremely profitable if you determine a few critical variables, and document them, from the beginning.

The balance of this paragraph assumes, at a minimum, the following basics: a discount in purchase price below intrinsic value, excellent management with transparency and integrity, a history of profit, and a moat (explained in more detail later in this chapter).

You need to know how you will receive a return on your investment. Will dividends be paid? What is the exit strategy? What level of control will you have? Remember that minority stakeholders may be subject to the whims of the majority if the formation and subsequent documents are not properly drafted. Further, even if you negotiate well and obtain rights that protect you, if you don't document them properly, the governing documents could be amended by the majority stakeholders and your rights could be flushed away before your eyes.

Insist upon distributions based upon certain milestones. Protect your rights by insisting upon certain voting provisions, including super majority provisions (perhaps 75 percent to 100 percent) prior to the amendment of certain rights that inure (are not) to your benefit, and have a documented exit strategy that can't be diluted or altered without your consent.

DEBT

Bonds are debt. Corporate paper is debt. Treasury bills (Tbills) are debt. Debt was probably issued by your city to light your streets. People invest in debt for several reasons, the most common of which are typically: debt has less risk than equity, it usually pays a fixed return, and in some instances such as certain forms of government bonds, the income is tax free. Debt is also a complex investment tool with multiple permutations which transcend the scope of this text.

Again, seek and obtain the advice of an expert prior to investing in this or any instrument you do not fully understand.

INSURANCE

Life Insurance. As an endowment tool, life insurance can be magical. Imagine a member of a church sowing between tithes and offerings, $10,000 last year. If the member is 75 years old and spends the next ten years in church giving the same amount, the church will receive $100,000. If the same member names the church as a beneficiary in an irrevocable policy of life insurance with a face amount of $250,000, the same funds could conceivably yield 250 percent of that sum for the church in the same amount of time. As a responsible steward for your business, church, or family, this tool should be considered as a viable method for estate and/or endowment planning in addition to prudent investing.

Types of Life Insurance. The main types of life insurance are term life insurance (no savings component), whole life insurance (a portion of your premiums goes into a savings account that is invested by the insurance company), and a variable life policy (the policy holder can, if the returns are positive, earn more on the invested funds while increasing the savings portion of the policy). Each type of policy has a death benefit which is the face amount, and each typically requires a monthly premium payment.

Premium amounts are adjusted based upon your health, age, medical history and other factors the underwriters accumulate (actuarial tables). As such, it is advisable to purchase insurance starting when you are younger so you can lock in a rate that is affordable. Further, though opinions differ widely, the authors suggest you acquire at least a portion of your insurance portfolio in whole life or variable policies so you can enjoy the savings component (which you can, if necessary for education or other needs, borrow tax free and offset against the death benefit).

While other types of insurance instruments, including annuities, exist and may be excellent tools for you, we again implore you to seek and obtain advice from experts who will, after carefully reviewing your individual circumstances, tailor a policy or policies to specifically meet the needs for you, your family, company, or church. Some estate planning aspects of life insurance are addressed in the Estate Planning section later in this chapter.

TOOLS

Beginning investors often invest in mutual funds as a method of diversifying to hedge their bets. Others day trade, buying and selling equities in an effort to capitalize on changes in the market (a highly speculative endeavor with high transaction costs). Sophisticated investors attempt to outperform the Standard & Poor's 500 Index, which is a scale designed to weigh the performance of 500 stocks of public companies traded on the New York Stock Exchange.

Regardless of your risk profile, fellowship is a core value you should exercise as you learn to invest in these volatile markets. Unless you are a professional or trained investor, you should hire a professional or, at a minimum, maintain a reasonably conservative risk profile. Never invest more than you can afford to lose and still maintain your current standard of living.

Follow the advice of Warren Buffett, the most successful investor in history, and do your homework—learn everything you can about everything you invest in, treat each investment as though you own the company or entity you are investing in, and be patient. Nothing is so good that it needs to be purchased immediately, and if you do not understand what you are buying intuitively, do not buy it. The same tools apply to the next class of investment to be discussed in the following pages, namely real estate.

Build a Moat. Invest in businesses and opportunities that are managed by people with integrity, intelligence, and energy. Also, ensure that your investment creates value for you. Determine this by barriers to entry in the industry in which you are investing, the level of brand awareness achieved by the sponsor, the track record of success demonstrated by the opportunity you are considering, and their dominance in the market segment in which they compete. Collectively, these factors form a *moat* which should protect your investment. Avoid investing in start-up entities unless there is some compelling reason to do so, particularly since it is preferable to invest in your own dreams at any stage than the fledgling dreams of another whose performance you have little understanding of and control over.

Kill the Noise. Day traders are affected by noise. Stock prices, economic forecasts, interest rates, and other short-term variables often cause them to take action, the sound business fundamentals of the companies in which they invest to the contrary notwithstanding. Turn off the television, put down the paper, and have faith in your well-informed investment decisions. Remember, never invest prior to doing deep homework, learning everything you can about anything you invest in, gaining through fellowship keen insights on the industry, company or opportunity, and then deciding if the investment is worth the risk. Will a short-term rate hike, stock price dip based on an industry scandal not involving your target, or other noise really adversely affect the fundamentals of your investment? Probably not, but following the irrational herd to the slaughter will. Kill the noise and have faith!

Believe in yourself. If you do the homework, seek and obtain fellowship with trusted advisors, plan well, and execute better, with discipline and your other core values, consistently applied, you, like Gideon, cannot and will not be defeated. With 300 men, Gideon defeated tens of thousands of men. You too can and will walk with God if you never abandon your faith and do your part.

REAL ESTATE

The real estate in mass merchant retailers (shelf space) is inundated with "get rich quick" books and tapes on real estate. Late night television, radio, and Internet media outlets are likewise pumping out content alleging to unlock the secrets of the get rich quick, real estate universe.

Have you ever received an envelope postmarked Heaven? It's probably a good idea not to wait for one. The myths of excess without personal sacrifice are as specious and pervasive as the lack of personal capital being an impregnable barrier to the acquisition of real property. Watch closely.

ANECDOTAL EVIDENCE

I remember purchasing my first property in 1989. I was in law school, and I had no money to speak of. I recognized, however, that my rent was equal to the amount of a mortgage I may have been able to obtain on a three bedroom condominium. The purchase price was $155,000 (a lot of money at the time), and I could only obtain an 80 percent loan. Initially,

I felt totally dejected because I could only scrape up $15,000 (another daunting task). How was I going to buy my dream home without the entire down payment?

Seller carry-back financing, though I had heard of it, was a legal concept with no practical application to my own life, so I thought at the time. When I realized that I had nothing to lose, I mustered the courage to ask the seller to carry back 10 percent of the purchase price so I could close the escrow.

Much to my surprise, the seller agreed, I located two roommates to live with me and help defray the mortgage expense, and I was shortly thereafter the owner of a nice new condominium in Tarzana, California. Since that date, we have used the seller carry-back technique to acquire many income-producing properties which, in turn, have generated significant wealth and cash flow.

Today, we house thousands of tenants in dozens and dozens of properties in multiple states and are aggressively looking to acquire more property every day. Remember, the moat in real estate is investing in businesses and opportunities that are managed by reputable people, and that your investment creates value for you. After learning all you can about the area in which you want to invest, determine barriers to entry, the track record of success demonstrated by the opportunity you are considering, and the uniqueness of the market.

BUYING INVESTMENT PROPERTY

Prosperity starts with a state of mind. Faith is the fundamental underpinning of success. Faith in God, your abilities, and the tools provided by others—borrowed science—are your starting points. Prosperity also requires hard work. You can achieve anything you desire, but your personal success depends largely on your willingness to commit, invest in yourself and your dream, and learn and apply that knowledge.

This chapter will lend you certain tools which, if applied properly and consistently, will guide you toward your goals. Specifically, we will be dealing with real estate investments, leverage, and financial management.

"I don't have the money to make the down payment." "I wasn't born rich." "I can barely stay above water." Did any of these thoughts cross your mind the last time you considered purchasing investment property? Do you still think doing so is beyond your reach? Are you waiting to "save enough?" *Stop waiting!*

We purchased one of our first apartment buildings in 1993. The combination of student loans, credit card debt, and a marginal FICO score made traditional leverage difficult, and we had little to no cash to work with. The property was a 24-unit apartment building in Los Angeles, California. Tax liens, structural issues, and our financial circumstances made the deal seem, at first blush, impossible. All we had was the desire to create wealth, the belief that, with perseverance, discipline, consistency, integrity, and the willingness to ask questions, learn and never quit, we could make the deal work.

We started by doing our homework. We wanted to know what the seller's sensitivities were—what, other than money, did they want or need? What, if anything, were they concerned about? We discovered, much to our surprise, that cash was not the major motivator of the seller. (As time went on, we applied this lesson repeatedly and obtained many good deals by remaining sensitive to the needs of sellers and by listening more and talking less.) We also learned that the property had delinquent property taxes, a lien from the county and problems with its foundation. The seller, a non-profit entity, was led by conservative trustees who viewed these issues as liabilities that transcended the benefits of owning the property. That, for a couple of investors in our 20s with no cash, credit, or experience, was our in.

Our continued research led us to the County Assessors Office where we discovered that, with a modest down payment, we could term out the property taxes for 60 months. Now we needed to tackle the structural issues with the building's foundation. We spoke with a few general contractors, and we promised the one we felt comfortable with that if he gave us a detailed bid at a reasonable price (which we determined after obtaining two other bids), we would give him the job if and when we acquired ownership and took possession. With these tools, we felt prepared to write an offer.

What had not changed since we discovered the opportunity was our lack of cash, credit, or experience. What *had* changed was our understanding of the seller's motivations and our understanding of how to craft an offer that would satisfy their needs. We wrote an offer for $250,000 which was $240,000 more than we had to spend; and the difference, our intended $10,000 down payment, was a total stretch. The accrued and unpaid property taxes were $140,000, so we asked the seller to carry-back paper—loan us $100,000 secured by a first deed of trust. We agreed to assume the property tax burden, and we offered to pay $10,000 in cash. Much to our surprise, the seller accepted our offer; we opened a 90-day escrow and began the process.

We sought the longer-than-necessary escrow period based upon the circumstances, principally because we had discovered during the process that we could repair our credit. We determined that with appropriate credit, we could refinance the property, pay off the taxes, repair the building and, with stabilized rents, create positive cash flow.

That is exactly what happened, except instead of refinancing the property for the exact sum of the taxes, the seller's loan and the repairs, ultimately, we took cash out and acquired another property. That property, which today is worth in excess of $2 million, is one of several dozen in our portfolio which extends from Southern and Central California to Portland, Oregon; Houston and Austin, Texas; Atlanta, Georgia; Boulder, Colorado; and, Duck, North Carolina. We also have, in various stages of development, nearly $200 million of mixed-use projects in several states.

Like you, we started with only the belief that we could do whatever we wanted to do if we kept swinging. While we have and continue to face challenges daily, our belief system and core values never change. We operate with discipline, integrity, and an unmitigated commitment to constant learning and growth. Our investors and stakeholders come first, we play fair, and we play to win.

HOMEOWNERSHIP

Now that you are in the process of enhancing your credit profile, preparing your budget, and reducing your expenses enough to save, within the budgeted time, a down payment, it is time to begin understanding the available tools. First-time homebuyers have multiple options to assist them in achieving the American dream of homeownership. From the Federal Housing Administration (FHA) and Fannie Mae (a federally backed mortgage provider), to funds available for educating those desirous of learning about purchasing their first home, your loan is out there waiting. Let's go find it.

A 2006 article revealed the repugnant truth that, on average, African-Americans and Latinos pay 30 percent more than their Caucasian counterparts for the same financial products.[1] Predatory lending remains pervasive. One of the seminal objectives of this book is to prevent you from being a victim of circumstance, deceit or a lack of knowledge, the latter being the prerequisite for the former.

With knowledge comes power, and the powerful are not typically victimized. Countrywide Financial was ordered to pay $3 million[2] toward education for those in minority classes after the revelation that, in certain instances, their borrowers were steered toward higher interest products; again, due to a lack of understanding.

DUPLEX NOT COMPLEX

Why not own your home and make money at the same time. One alternative to acquiring investment property and increasing your cash flow and/or spreading your expenses over multiple income streams is the acquisition of a two to four-unit complex. This type of property will still qualify as a primary residence, and you are permitted to write off against ordinary income interest on up to $1.1 million in residential debt. You will also, unlike a standard residence, be allowed to depreciate the property (divide the value of the building, as determined by the assessor or your purchase price, by its useful life as determined by the Internal Revenue Service (IRS)—typically 28 years) and use this expense to offset income earned from renting out the units you do not occupy.

Properly structured, this type of investment could allow you to purchase your first property and pay less as your contribution to your mortgage than you are paying in rent. Finally, if you are in fact a first-time homebuyer, you may be eligible for special financing, including FHA guaranteed loans which may allow you to borrow up to 95 percent of the purchase price.

Assume you are living in a three bedroom apartment that rents for $1,200 per month. You are reading the real estate section of the newspaper because you have decided to immerse yourself in an asset class in which you are interested in investing. You locate an apartment building with four units priced at $1.2 million. You contact a loan broker and find out that you can obtain a 95 percent loan which requires mortgage payments of $6,500 per month, interest only.

Each unit in the complex is renting for $1,500 per month. At first blush, it appears that living in the building will cost you more than living in your apartment. But after you calculate the $24,000 interest deduction from your income taxes, even in the 30 percent tax bracket, you save another $8,000 on your income taxes per year. With no more math, you purchased a substantial asset and are servicing the debt for approximately $100 more than you were paying for an apartment. If you get the seller to help you with the down payment, separately meter the property so your tenants pay their own utilities, and install a coin-operated laundry system, you end up ahead of the game.

DIVERSIFICATION

The level of diversification that is appropriate is a hotly debated topic. Mutual funds are open-end funds that are not listed for trading on a stock exchange and are issued by companies which use their capital to invest in other companies. Mutual funds sell their own new shares to investors and buy back their old shares upon redemption. Capitalization is not fixed and normally shares are issued as people want them. Mutual funds are a well-accepted method for equity diversification. Debt funds likewise exist.

While some diversification makes intuitive sense to hedge against down turns in a segment of the economy or otherwise, investing in sound companies, be it in the form of debt or equity, good properties in the right locations, and appropriate financial products managed by good companies run by intelligent, energetic managers, makes sense. And if those investments perform, betting big on them likewise makes sense.

The best investment, bar none, remains an investment in you. Invest deeply in yourself. Buy an education before you buy a share of stock. Reinvest in your business if you have built it with integrity and discipline, and if you have acquired industry knowledge and surrounded yourself with experts who round you out and operate in faith. If you did and/or do so, others will follow.

ESTATE PLANNING

Estate planning is a necessary step in ensuring your financial legacy and the prosperity of your heirs. Put your estate in order, lead by example, and teach your flock, employees and heirs the principles of sound financial stewardship. "Train a child in the way he should go, and when he is old he will not turn from it" (Prov. 22:6). Start planning early.

Multiple tools exist for the purpose of estate planning. This is an extremely complex area of the law, and the decisions you make can have significant tax and other impacts on your estate and heirs. Seek counsel, including legal, business, and financial advice. This section briefly discusses some fundamental mechanisms at your disposal, including the inter vivos trust (living trust), the family limited partnership life insurance trust, the generation-skipping trust and, for asset protection purposes, the irrevocable trust.

THE INTER VIVOS TRUST

The inter vivos or living trust is essentially a contract, entitled a trust, which, if properly drafted and executed, causes the transfer of assets from the trustor (you) to the trust. The trustee is the person or entity appointed by you and enumerated in the trust to act as a fiduciary (a person with a special duty of care) to the ultimate recipient, the beneficiary (ostensibly your heirs or other designees like your church).

Title to properties, stocks, and any other asset you, as trustor, decide to convey, gets transferred by deed, assignment, or other mechanism, to the trust. This form of trust is revocable by the trustor for any or no reason, and as such, it offers little if any true asset protection from valid creditors. It does, however, allow your heirs and designees to avoid the cost, both in terms of time and money, of probate. Special considerations when forming this type of trust include the care you must use when designating a trustee. Make sure this person or entity is capable of managing the assets and hopefully contributing to an increase in their intrinsic value; and make sure your confidence is well-placed. Do your homework.

FAMILY LIMITED PARTNERSHIP

This entity is formed exactly as any other limited partnership is formed. Generally, an individual who would have otherwise acted as trustor if a trust were to be set up, either personally, or preferably, through a corporate entity, acts as general partner and the heirs act as limited partners. The benefits of this form include asset protection against valid creditors, a discount in value of the property contributed if properly handled which, in turn, can act to reduce estate taxes and the ability for you, as the controlling stakeholder of the general partner, to retain control over the assets during your life or for as long as you want.

LIFE INSURANCE TRUST

You can transfer life insurance you acquire to a life insurance trust; and your beneficiaries can, if properly formed, enjoy additional protections for the ultimate proceeds from the policy or policies. Additionally, probate can also be avoided by and through the use of this vehicle.

ENDNOTES

1. "Minorities pay more for mortgages—Trade group challenges study's findings; credit quality at issue," by Amy Hoak, *MarketWatch*. Last Update: 6:02 PM ET, May 31, 2006. Accessed at: http://www.marketwatch.com/News/Story/Story.aspx?guid=%7B29B2B166-7A4E-4D02-9428-CF2227DF6D87%7D&siteid=google.

2. "Seven Defendants Sentenced in Mortgage Fraud Scheme," February 22, 2007. Found on Website: http://www.usdoj.gov/usao/mss/feb2207_wed.html.

Forming and Shepherding a Nonprofit Organization

CHAPTER NINE

Formation and Structure

STRUCTURING THE ENTITY

Remember, your vision will keep you focused on your goals and keep you from diverting time and energy from your core mission. Never forget that good intentions and enthusiasm do not guarantee financial or other success— hard work and believing in your God-given gifts will.

There are three types of nonprofit organizations: religious, public, and mutual. To be tax exempt, a nonprofit organization must qualify under one of the categories of exempt organizations. Exemption from income or franchise tax is a statutory privilege; it is not automatically recognized or granted.

Therefore, a nonprofit corporation is generally taxed as a corporation under Internal Revenue Code (IRC) Section 11 and Revenue and Tax Code Sections 23151 and 23501 unless it establishes a specific exemption with the Internal Revenue Service (IRS) or with the state in which you file. The most familiar of these categories is the "charitable" exemption under IRC 501(c)(3).

IS THE ENTITY NECESSARY?

If you haven't already, ask yourself these questions that will help formulate your intent.

1. What purpose will be served by forming the entity?

2. Does a need exist?

3. Whose need are you trying to address?

4. Which other entities are in the space and can you and your team really serve the need you have identified?

5. How will you finance that service?

NONPROFIT AND TAXABLE

Forming a nonprofit does not equate to tax exempt status. Nonprofit organizations may have to pay taxes. The formation of an entity starts with the vision statement and is followed up with filing the Articles of Incorporation. In the context of nonprofit entity formation, however, in parity with the creation of the vision is taking time to think through the business, in addition to the purpose, of the entity in tangible terms. Questions you need to answer include:

1. What are the intended sources of funding?

2. What is the anticipated growth rate?

3. Revenue?

4. Number of employees?

5. Does your vision actually require the formation of a nonprofit?

6. What portion of your revenue will ultimately be taxable regardless of the type of entity you form?

Since, pursuant to IRC Section 11 and Revenue and Taxation Code, Sections 23151 and 23501, most nonprofits are and remain taxable, you need to understand clearly which bucket your revenue should appropriately spill into and whether, in addition to the nonprofit, a for-profit entity is appropriate. Absent a specific exemption to the previously cited code sections, the formation of a nonprofit does you no good. The most common exemption remains IRC Section 501(c)(3). This is called the charitable exemption.

THREE TYPES OF NONPROFIT ORGANIZATIONS

The three basic types of nonprofit organizations are 1) faith-based; 2) public benefit; and 3) mutual benefit. This book will focus primarily on the faith-based nonprofit organization, but a majority of the principles discussed are applicable between entity types.

SOUND BUSINESS PLAN AND FINANCIAL VIABILITY

After you have determined that there is a need and you have the vision to start a nonprofit, the next logical step is organization. Organization is the key to the implementation of the vision. Without an organization to carry out the vision there will be no success. Here are some key questions to ask at this stage:

1. Is there a business plan?

2. Who will administer the enterprise on a daily basis?

3. Are qualified and interested directors available?

4. Are the directors willing to make the commitment necessary for a successful enterprise?

5. What is the projected budget?

6. How will the necessary resources be raised?

7. What are the long-range plans for financing the enterprise?

Tax Exemption

A tax-exempt organization can make a profit, and many do. A nonprofit organization may be a taxable entity and therefore not have tax-exempt status. Although most nonprofits wish to be exempt from income tax, occasionally an entity will not qualify for tax exempt status or may not wish to be subject to the benefits and burdens of tax exemption but still have sound reasons to be established as a nonprofit corporation.

Public Benefit – Mutual Benefit – Faith-based

This text will focus primarily on faith-based nonprofit organizations, but for comparison, other types of nonprofit organizations include public benefit organizations such as hospitals or research facilities (IRC, Section 509(A)) and mutual benefit nonprofit organizations, including foundations and certain trusts.

To Tax or Not to Tax?

Congratulations! You formed your church, you received your stamped Articles of Incorporation back from the Secretary of State, and your tax exempt designation was mailed to you by the IRS. You purchased a building, you are holding services, selling books, tapes, and Internet subscriptions, and you are receiving tithes and offerings. All is well, and all of the income is tax free, right? *Wrong!*

Not all of your income will be tax free. First, product sales require the calculation and remittance of sales tax to the local taxing authorities. Second, your state needs to provide you with a determination letter. Finally, if, for example, you sold some real property, like any activity outside your core business approved as tax exempt by the taxing authorities, the sale would be subject to taxation.

FOR-PROFIT ORGANIZATION

If your business plan reveals that certain activities you will engage in may be subject to taxation, consider the formation of another entity that will be a for-profit organization intending to pay tax. If you evangelize outside of your church, have the honorariums paid to the for-profit. Create an arms-length, fair arrangement between the entities, wherein the church will purchase product from the for-profit at wholesale, sell the product at retail, and keep the difference. The for-profit entity will pay income tax on the wholesale profit, the nonprofit will pay sales tax, and the arrangement reduced to a writing and blessed by both boards, will be legitimate.

ORGANIZE IN WHICH STATE OR COUNTRY?

Jurisdiction of any entity, nonprofit or otherwise, is a critical decision. The laws of each state differ greatly, and the activities reflected in your plan may be to the detriment of your organization if you form it in a particular state.

Back to fellowship. Hire the best lawyer and consultant you can find. Most people incorporate in the state in which they live or where their church is. Why is that? While faith in God is never blind, decisions without knowledge are not fortified by Scripture. Your mission statement drives your plan and, your plan will define and emanate from, reciprocally, the jurisdiction you choose.

Remember, you can be in one state, incorporate in another, and do business in any other. You need to qualify where you do business, but that notwithstanding, your personal location is not the driver.

STRUCTURING THE ENTITY

IRC Section 501(c)(3), describes the most widely known nonprofit entity. Many faith-based nonprofit entities are formed under this IRC Section. While others, including certain trusts, foundations, ministries, and related nonprofit entities exist, the nonprofit discussion in this text will be relegated to the IRC Section 501(c)(3).

Formation

Your faith-based nonprofit begins with the choice of a name. Depending upon the jurisdiction (state) in which you choose to form your entity, you will begin the process by reserving a name with the Secretary of State. After the name is reserved and confirmed with a registration verification from the Secretary of State, the *Articles of Incorporation* (the "Articles") are prepared.

The Articles define the type of entity and its purpose. The Articles may, but need not, define prohibited purposes. Articles range in complexity from one page to dozens of pages. Further, if your entity is affiliated with a parent organization, the articles may reference and incorporate that organization and its articles, bylaws, or charter.

The Articles can be as simple as one page and as complex and verbose as a novel. Depending upon the reason for the formation of the relevant entity, the Articles may contain restrictive or expansive provisions; for example, prohibitions against gambling and alcohol distribution for faith-based nonprofit organizations. Conversely, language reflecting the ability of the shareholders to transact "any and all lawful business" within the for-profit entity is typical.

In either event, at a minimum, the Articles should outline the purpose for which the entity was created. Historically, the Articles would also, in many states, define the lifespan of the entity. Today, corporations are almost always formed with perpetual existence contemplated by the incorporators, and as such, the Articles are silent as to duration. Within the corporate scheme, multiple choices remain.

The *Bylaws* of a corporation, nonprofit or otherwise, are, as they sound, comprised of the "laws" of the entity. Unlike the Articles, the Bylaws are the rules and regulations that guide the entity. Standard provisions include timing of meetings, the number of members necessary to take action on behalf of the entity (often referred to as the quorum), the notice required for a meeting, the number of votes necessary to take action on behalf of the entity, election procedures for officers and directors, provisions relating to the acquisition and/or disposition of assets, and all other operational features you and the founding members desire to define, within the confines of state and federal laws relating to nonprofit entities.

An important distinction between Bylaws and Articles is the fact that only Articles are recorded and maintained as a public record. As such, any amendment requires an amendment to a public document. Bylaws, on the other hand, can be amended pursuant to the procedures set forth therein. Further, you may have operational reasons to refrain from having certain issues be of public record. Definitely seek and obtain the advice of competent counsel when drafting these critical documents.

Statement By Domestic Non-Profit. The Secretary of State typically requires a Statement By Domestic Non-Profit Corporation (the "Statement") be filed (either annually or once every two years depending upon your state of incorporation), identifying the agent for service of process (the "Agent"), officers and directors, the address and other salient information relating to your entity. The Statement usually must be accompanied by a fee. Waivers may be available based upon hardship.

The Agent designated in the Statement is designated as an alternate recipient of official documentation, including the service of lawsuits, documentation from public and private organizations, tax information and any other official correspondence. Any change in the address of the Agent or any other information in the Statement usually requires the preparation and filing of an amended Statement.

Choose someone outside your organization to serve as Agent. Professional organizations exist for this purpose. Your organization's general counsel can likewise act as your Agent for service of process. Irrespective of your choice of agents, ensure that a concise protocol exists if and when legal process is served upon your organization. Always consult your counsel and appropriate advisors, and depending upon the exigency and seriousness of the claim or claims, consider informing your board. Finally, most standard insurance policies require you to notify your carrier of potential liability at your earliest reasonable opportunity. Include an insurance tender protocol when dealing with legal documents.

IRS FORM SS-4

Your taxpayer identification number, also known as your employer identification number (EIN) is obtained after you file the Articles. Since obtaining tax exempt status from the IRS takes time, you will, immediately following receipt of your approved Articles, file the Statement and obtain your EIN. You will need to complete the SS-4 form, it is simple and self-explanatory. You can obtain your EIN over the telephone, through the Internet, or by mail. As with all key corporate documentation, maintain this form in a safe place. This is the principal identification number for your organization and will be used often.

STATE OF FORMATION

Certain states are preferred by certain professionals in choosing where to form your entity. While this advice is rooted in divergent opinion for multiple reasons beyond the scope of this text, since your entity will, in all likelihood, not be sold, may not be merged, and hopefully, will exist for a very long time, as long as you adhere to the state and federal laws, you may well decide to incorporate in the state in which your efforts will be significantly expended. This logic does not, in all instances, extend to your for-profit entity or entities. Issues to consider include capital access, rules and regulations regarding state income tax, state laws regarding shareholder, officer and director liability and a myriad of other issues.

CHAPTER TEN

Types of Entities

To make informed decisions about forming an organization, you need to familiarize yourself with the different types of entities. Brief descriptions follow—more information can be found on the Web, at your local library, or through your counsel or consultant.

C CORPORATION

The most common type of entity in the United States today remains the C Corporation. This entity, like those discussed below, offers the protection of having a corporate shell; and basically, the corporation is deemed a separate legal person for liability purposes. As such, as long as you adhere to the corporate formalities (which are codified and differ from state to state), have meetings, the appropriate officers, directors, capitalization, and minutes, the debts, liabilities, and exposure from doing business in and through this entity should not inure personal detriment.

Specifically, if your corporation gets sued and a judgment is entered against it, done right, you will not suffer from personal liability. If, however, you fail to adhere to the corporate formalities, the entity will be deemed your alter ego, the legal distinction between you and your corporation will be collapsed, and you will be held legally responsible for all of its liabilities, past, present, and future. Knowledge first, then discipline, will help you avoid this draconian result.

One problem with the C Corporation is the risk of double taxation. Corporations get taxed at the corporate level, and any profits then distributed get taxed at the individual level. As such, the risk of double taxation is a real one and the impetus for the statutory creation of the following types of entities. Beyond double taxation, losses are also trapped in C Corporations which, once you make profit elsewhere, will not be allowed as an offset against anything other than gains and profits within the same corporation. Like all corporations, for-profit, non-profit, Subchapter C or S, these entities are formed by filing Articles of Incorporation with the Secretary of State in the appropriate jurisdiction.

As a general rule in the formation of entities, less is more regarding publicly filed documents. The operational gravamen (the most substantial part of a charge or an accusation) of these entities is contained in the bylaws, the rules of conduct for the corporation and in the Shareholders' Agreement, the rules of conduct for the shareholders vis a vis one another and the corporation. These documents are not public, and consequently, for many reasons, they are the preferred venue for salient, privileged information regarding the company and its shareholders. Nonprofit formation documents, conversely, can be construed as public documents in certain circumstances.

S Corporation

A Subchapter S Corporation offers the same liability protections as a C Corporation, but unlike its cousin, its shareholders are treated as partners for taxation purposes. It is a pass through entity that "passes through" all of its profits and losses to the shareholders. While numerous other tax and corporate considerations exist in determining the type of entity to use, in most instances when the end game is not going public, S Corporations and other pass through entities are preferable to C Corporations.

LIMITED LIABILITY COMPANIES AND PARTNERSHIPS

Limited liability companies are now thoroughly accepted and authorized in all states. They too are pass through entities (though one can elect to treat them otherwise). They offer the same protection as corporations, and often they are preferred because they do not have the same degree of formality associated with their use, thus reducing the chance of an alter ego determination by a Court.

Limited liability partnerships are relegated to use by professional organizations such as lawyers and accountants. This distinction without a difference is the only one that in any way differentiates the two. These entities are formed by the simple filing of forms LLC1 and LLP1, entitled articles of organization, respectively, with the appropriate secretary of state. The critical internal documents that govern these entities and their stakeholders, called members versus shareholders, are entitled operating agreements. These, like Bylaws, contain issues ranging from voting rights to the replenishment of negative capital accounts.

LIMITED PARTNERSHIPS

Limited partnerships were created to afford investors partnership benefits along with the protection afforded to shareholders. They were also formed as investment vehicles designed to attract capital investment by a broad investor base. Basically, in most instances, a type of corporate entity, be it a C Corporation, limited liability company or other form, assumes the role of general partner. The general partner (there can be more than one) is responsible for all decisions made by the limited partnership, and limited partners are prohibited from exercising any influence over the operations (the penalty being the loss of corporate protection if they violate this rule). The limited partners' only exposure to liability, similar to the exposure of a member of a limited liability company, is the amount of money they invested in the partnership, assuming they adhere to the statutory formalities.

The general partner, like any partner, is totally exposed, thus the corporate form. This type of entity is formed by the filing of an LP1, entitled a Certificate of Limited Partnership, with the appropriate secretary of state. The salient, non-public document that governs the conduct of this entity form and its partners is a Limited Partnership Agreement. Copies if the LP1 and Limited Partnership Agreement can be found on the Urban Website.

Remember the concept of fellowship and the wisdom surrounding seeking and obtaining the advice of experts prior to choosing the type of entity in which to conduct your business. After you obtain the appropriate expert legal, tax, and business advice, your next step is to form the entity and begin the journey.

CHAPTER ELEVEN

Organization

ORGANIZING A NONPROFIT ORGANIZATION

You will begin your organization by drafting the organizational documents known as Bylaws. The Bylaws establish the procedures for governing and operating the organization's activities and conduct. They serve three purposes: to provide rules for matters not covered by statute/law; to alter specific default rules that are controlled by statute/law in the absence of a contrary Bylaw; and to provide a ready reference to the governing laws and rules for the organization's attorney, directors, and officers.

WHY A NONPROFIT ORGANIZATION?

Nonprofit entities are subject to higher scrutiny, more oversight, and are more restrictive in terms of compensation for officers and stakeholders. While the decision to form one emanates appropriately from the vision, many people often believe that all mission-oriented businesses should be nonprofits. If your primary driver is the avoidance of federal and/or state income tax, you are making the wrong decision!

EXEMPT OR NONEXEMPT

Many people think that nonprofit organizations are tax exempt upon formation. *Wrong!* Without falling within one of the following categories and successfully applying for tax exempt status federally and on the state level, *you will owe taxes*. If not filed correctly, in addition to all back taxes, interest and penalties (upon which additional interest is calculated) will be also assessed. At the risk of being redundant, exemption from income or franchise tax is a statutory privilege. It is not automatically recognized or granted.

Therefore, a nonprofit organization is generally taxed as a corporation under IRC 11 and Revenue and Tax Code sections 23151 and 23501 unless it establishes a specific exemption with the IRS and in the state where you have filed. Check with your own state tax officials. The most common exemption is the "charitable" exemption under IRC 501(c)(3). Faith-based nonprofit organizations fit under this exemption (as do many others).

A Nonprofit Entity?

The following 11 questions, and others, should help guide you in determining whether your Statement should come alive in a nonprofit or for-profit entity.

1. Are the founders willing to allow the organization to be operated under the direction of a board of directors that may take the organization in a direction the founders would not approve of and maybe even remove the founders entirely?

While the appropriate drafting of the Bylaws should limit the leader's exposure to being ousted, the members remain the main stakeholders; and candidly, if they want you out, first, you should already know it and be gone, and if not, the statutory scheme vests them with the immutable right and power to unseat you. Corporate structure is, after all, rooted thematically in a democratic model where the ultimate vote, and hence power, rests with the stakeholders and shareholders. If you can't handle this heat, stay out of the faith-based nonprofit kitchen, and evangelize as a sole proprietor.

2. Is nonprofit status important for obtaining special treatment in a particular area? For example, will it be important for the organization to qualify for reduced-rate mailing privileges, for exemption from unemployment insurance, and for exemption from federal securities registration? How about property tax exemptions, housing allowance exemptions for the leader, and the exemption from income tax?

3. Will outside funding, such as grants, depend on nonprofit status? Is it important to be able to raise equity capital from investors? If so, what regulations will apply? Who will raise the money?

This is where it gets a bit interesting. The First Amendment to the United States Constitution contains the Establishment Clause within which rests the separation of church and state doctrine. With literally billions of federal dollars earmarked to mission activities, is your nonprofit the right type of nonprofit to apply for and receive those funds? Do you need to set up another nonprofit, say an Economic Development Corporation (EDC) to access that money?

4. Will qualified and motivated directors be more easily attracted to serve if the enterprise is nonprofit? For officers and managers, will a salary be adequate incentive or will stock incentives be important?

5. Is the client aware that more rigorous investment standards may be applied to a nonprofit enterprise or that the enterprise may be subject to supervision by the Attorney General?

6. Will it be difficult for the nonprofit enterprise to keep up with the paperwork required by the IRS and the Franchise Tax Board?

7. Will the rules against distributions by nonprofit corporations and the inurement of benefits to an individual cause problems?

8. Does the client anticipate engaging in transactions with related parties that would violate applicable federal tax rules (private foundation self-dealing rules or public charity intermediate sanction rules)?

9. Will the requirement that the organization serve a public purpose and the prohibition against serving a private purpose create problems?

10. If a product is to be marketed, will people be more likely to buy from an organization that has nonprofit status? Will sales tax be charged regardless of the type of entity?

11. Will the very limited sales tax differences between profit and nonprofit groups be important?

These questions and others should be asked by you and the advisors you seek and obtain should help you decide which matter. Not every missioned-activity fits into a nonprofit organization. By way of example, if you preach outside of your organization for money, we suggest you take that income into a for-profit entity and pay tax on those honorariums. Certain product sales, service income, and investment income should likewise fall within for profit activities relegated to entities of that character.

MISSION, VISION, AND VALUES

After you have decided if the entity will be nonprofit or for-profit, the first step in building an organization, no matter how small or large, is to establish and write a *mission statement*. Every organization has *a reason for being* and this should be articulated in a mission statement. The mission statement sets all other priorities within the organization. The mission statement outlines what needs you are attempting to meet and what values will guide you in meeting those needs. This corporate strategy is what links the mission statement with the personal objectives followed by employees.

To do this, elicit words, phrases, and ideas from everyone within the ranks, then condense those thoughts into a simple paragraph, free of jargon. Make sure the mission statement answers these three questions:

1. What are the needs we exist to address?

2. What are we doing to address those needs?

3. What principles guide our work?

DEFINING THE VISION

Defining the *vision* of your organization includes setting goals for where you want to go and objectives for how to get there.

Well chosen goals will keep you pointed in the right direction for as long as your organization exists. Goals are your road map for the future and should be carefully defined.

Organizations that lack vision are doomed to failure as the competition moves a step ahead, following their objectives to reach their goals.

CREATING A VALUES STATEMENT

What principles are behind the scenes of your organization guiding you and the way you operate? Announce these to the world through your *values statement*. You will find it to be invaluable, especially when you face a crisis. It is then when your true set of beliefs will be tested. Adhering to your values can both boost your image and the success of your organization.

KEY POINTS ON WHICH TO BUILD

There are key strategies and values that go into building every organization. Attention to detail is important. Having a strategy is critical. If you don't aim at something you will miss it every time.

1. Establish Your Shared Values

Every organization has a set of values, whether they're spelled out or implicit, that control how it functions. These values establish the core culture of the organization. Employees who don't fit within the corporate culture will eventually depart. It is critical that management and employees share the same values. These values must then be communicated in word and action to those who interact at every level with the organization.

2. Establish and Execute Your Strategy

The execution of a good strategy is at least as important as having that strategy in the first place. Before an organization begins to function, it must first establish a strategy to accomplish its goals. There must be a balance of establishment and execution of strategies. An organization with no strategy but excellent execution may, in fact, be better off than a company with a good strategy that is badly implemented.

Your established strategy provides you the ability to measure your execution. It is important that you have established strategies that you can use to measure success. Part of the strategy is the establishment of a management group through the review of their performance against tangible deliverables. Part of an effective strategy is focused and efficient communication between management and employees. This communication should flow in both directions. Management must be able to direct the flow of the employee and resolve problems in accomplishing its goals. Conversely, the employee must be free to communicate to management any obstacles or issues that they encounter in the implementation of the goals.

3. Data and Process Standardization

For a new organization, it's not enough to introduce an aligned strategy, define the mission statement of the organization, and identify the organization's core values. Processes and procedures must also be efficient. Limited resources must be leveraged to maximize their value. At the very least, the organization must strive to become more efficient structurally than its competition. This is possible only if best practices, processes, and systems are recognized throughout the organization and if every part of the company follows a common business model. Very few companies realize this ideal.

The church provides an excellent example of leverage and opportunity. Six days a week, the building is dark. Others pay hundreds of dollars per week, per child, for daycare. Isn't it intuitive that most parents would prefer to leave their children with those they trust and share their values? Now for the leverage. Forty kids at $600.00 per month equates to $24,000 per month in additional income with no additional rental expense. Proper planning, efficient execution, and leverage are sacrosanct principles.

Management processes and systems can be standardized only if the correct data is available to evaluate their effectiveness.

4. Agility Is Key

An abundance of research suggests that most organizations fail to execute strategies designed to improve their position in the market because the external environment changes faster than strategies can be devised and implemented. This is called strategic obsolescence. High-performance organizations achieve a high level of agility so they can identify change and respond optimally—or, even better, set the pace for change within their industry.

There are three primary ways to create agility in an organization. One is by centralizing processes, data, and systems companywide. This demands that you have a highly effective IT department that will implement appropriate technologies. A second method for improving agility is through smart sourcing. Standardizing as many product components as possible and using subcontractors to produce and deliver those components can lead to a dramatic decrease in new product development time, and a faster response to market trends.

Project-based management can improve an organization's agility. If corporate functions such as human resources can be fluidly deployed as needed by strategic initiatives, rather than being housed within rigid departmental structures, teams can be formed and dissolved more rapidly to pounce on opportunities or respond to threats.

Regardless of the depth and sophistication of your mission, vision, values, and strategic plan, at the beginning and end of the day, it comes down to the people. Do you have the right people in the right seats? Do you intimately understand your target (customer, investor, banker, congregant)? Are you providing what they want or what you want them to want?

IDEO is a leading product and technology think tank in San Francisco, California. They were hired to determine the commercial and consumer viability of a simple technology designed to test and repair cell phones. The owners of the technology intended to abandon it because adults in multiple focus groups thought text messaging was burdensome and not user friendly. The team at IDEO decided to test text messaging on the "zero twenty" group of youth. The rest is history!

Had the proprietor not sought fellowship with those capable of expanding and exploring the test base, this opportunity would have been lost. Understand the target and let your market pull, rather than push what you seek to provide. If you have to push too hard, provide something else.

ESTABLISHING A BUSINESS PLAN

No organization can achieve goals it fails to set. People are no different. Plan the work, and work the plan. You, as the shepherd of your organization, must effectively plan the utilization and multiplication of your organization's resources. You have a fiduciary and scriptural obligation to do so.

The term *business plan* is viewed with particular suspicion in the faith-based nonprofit realm where we often hear complaints that, in their simplest form, sound similar to, "This is church, not a business. Those principles do not apply here." Our response is equally simple, clear, and consistent. The faith-based nonprofit organization and its leadership collectively have a fiduciary duty to responsibly shepherd the hard-earned, after-tax resources voluntarily offered and sown by its membership. The business of the faith-based nonprofit is required in order to fortify and support rather than desecrate and replace the ecclesiastical mandate.

Distilled to its essence, an anointed messenger with a relevant message and no members is analogous to a For Sale sign in the middle of the desert. A full house with no cash management tools and systems is not sustainable. Absent investment, endowment, and planned giving strategies, a succession plan is little more than a job offer. Again, absent prosperity, there is little opportunity for philanthropy, and hard work is not the singular solution. Plan the work and then work the plan.

The fundamental components of a business plan include: the mission or vision statement (which encompasses mission, vision and values), a budget (which should include or complement a sources and uses of funds analysis), a marketing plan, strategic plan, and a critical path.

BUDGET

In the context of a faith-based nonprofit, the budget transcends money. Clearly, not every auxiliary will be profitable. We suggest a bottom up approach first in this process. Have each team leader (those in charge of each department, section, ministry, auxiliary, committee, etc.) prepare and present a draft document outlining their intended activities for the year, their expectation regarding necessary funding, their hope regarding the source for that funding and any revenue opportunities associated therewith. Also have them identify how their activities comport with the vision. Ultimately, to prevent an auxiliary from seeking a $1,000 gift from Wells Fargo for your singles ministry, when your daycare facility was successfully negotiating for $50,000, budgeting, planned giving, and all financial aspects of your organization, short-, middle- and long-term, must be centralized.

Essentially, have your leaders budget how many new members their activities will garner; for example, how many singles will be introduced through the singles ministry. Budgets are not only economic. After each group prepares their plan, they must debate its respective veracity and accuracy. Negotiate with your leadership and ensure that they take ownership of their numbers. It is through this process only that performance goals will be achieved. If you tell people what you want them to do, at best, they will deliver the minimum. If you ask them what they think they can accomplish, you will be amazed by the results. God is devoid of limitations. Why limit His children?

Ultimately the budget should be a real stretch to achieve, but it must be achievable. Make sure the goals rationally relate to the resources available to achieve them. That is your responsibility as the leader.

MARKETING PLAN

Once you aggregate the plans into one overall budget, it is time for execution. One element of that execution will be marketing. As such, the budgets of each group will necessarily require some element of marketing. Their marketing efforts should come through one central portal so replication and waste are avoided.

One distinction between secular and nonsecular organizations and activities is the qualitative criteria for success. A church with 20 new members per week may very well be considered successful while a retail operation with 20 new visitors and no incremental sales growth may not.

Consequently, marketing efforts for nonprofit organizations are geared, like their for-profit counterparts, toward the vision/mission/values of the organization. Are we saving more souls? Are we increasing the Body? Are we spreading the Word? These traditional questions and their traditional answers remain relevant today.

Essentially, the Word has not changed. The method of spreading it, however, has changed dramatically; and while some traditional assemblies view the change and its rapidity with disdain, don't fall into that trap. Your organization has never had a better opportunity to pervasively expand throughout the world than today. Your physical space is no longer a barrier, and as such, the modern world and technology stand as true testaments to the inability to bind God.

INTERNET MARKETING

You have a growing 100-member church in a 300-seat edifice. Your budget is tight, your sermons are too; and you know that when people hear your message, they are touched and remain members of your congregation. You also know that your anointing will not, without marketing, reach all who are in need.

While preparing your budget, you realize that $5,000 remains available for marketing. Your research reveals that a direct mail piece, even with your nonprofit mailing rate, would yield approximately a 2 percent response (maybe less). While those 50 people who actually respond may, at some ratio, convert to members, you have expended your entire budget for marketing with the hopes of some response and no hope of recidivism, that is, repeated messaging to create an indelible impression in the minds of those seeing your message.

If, however, you created an e-devotional, essentially an electronic message with your voice, passion, and anointing revealed therein, you may be able to reach 500,000 people for the same price in 100,000-person increments, five times. Now you have exposed a much broader base to multiple messages rather than exposing a narrow base to a mono-dimensional postcard which reveals none of your gifts. Further, once you have e-mail addresses and the appropriate technology, the cost to remarket is minimal. We will explore these concepts further in future texts. Suffice it to say that marketing is an essential element of 21st century church and the duty of the faith-based nonprofit leadership to both steward the congregational resources as well as to spread the Word.

STRATEGIC PLAN

Goals that aren't set, aren't met. Your strategic plan is the implementation path for your organization. It is the who, how, when, and where of your business plan. Why not "why" you ask? Your missions statement already answered that question. Let's break it down together.

Who?

Success requires accountability. Budgets and financial reports force accountability, but absent linear responsibility being vested in particular people, who do we hold accountable for the success and/or failure of the organization? If you can't answer this question, you do not have a plan. A single person must ultimately be responsible for each goal. That does not mean that person needs to do all the work. It simply means we will hold one team leader responsible for each task.

Since each goal should be designed to advance the vision, the people responsible should be selected based upon their respective skill sets. Specifically, don't place those with financial genius in marketing. Do not place those with blind ambition and a desire to accumulate personal wealth in finance. To repeat Jim Collins in *Good to Great*, we need the right people on the bus, and those people need to be in the right seats. The right people in the wrong seats are no better than hiring the wrong people and expecting positive results.

Every "deliverable" must ultimately rest at the feet of one person who must likewise be responsible to someone or some other people. Since the business plan itself will ultimately be blessed by the leader and ratified by the board, ultimately, those the board serves—the members or shareholders as the case may be, bless the plan and either benefit by its implementation or are damaged by a lack of it.

How?

The gravamen of your plan is an answer to this question. How are we going to increase membership? Through a variety of venues including Internet marketing, a health fair, sponsorship, grant writing, evangelizing, etc. These elements of the strategic plan are the guts of forward progress. Each element must, as set forth above, be budgeted, not only in terms of financial impact and resource allocation, but also in terms of how we quantify success.

Absent these elements, our downstream reporting matrix will be useless. Again, nothing measured, nothing gained. Once the goals are set, you must answer how they will be achieved, and each responsible "who" must buy into the solutions. You can't hold people responsible for achieving your goals if you are the only one who wants them reached. You must have shared goals they also own before they will truly take responsibility for working toward achieving the goals.

When?

You need a critical path. This will delineate milestones that must be reached on a timeline. If you set a goal of doubling membership and unleash your team with all the tools to accomplish that goal, ten years from now when they achieve the goal, will you be satisfied? Yes, if their omniscience allowed them to know that your time horizon was ten years. No, if you failed to tell them you expected the goal to be reached in one. There is no viable plan without the critical path.

Where?

This element is really subsumed in the "how" part of the strategic plan. Here is an example most faith-based leaders miss. You preach on Sunday, and you do it very well. You pack the house, and you have three sermons per day. You're tired. Your deacons suggest a fourth service to increase revenue.

First, overworking the star player on any team is not a sustainable solution. Second, your team has still failed to leverage its fixed assets appropriately. What are you doing with the sanctuary the other six days? How about a daycare facility? A filming location? A community meeting hall? You could rent these locations from others ("where") or rent them to others ("how") in order to achieve your goals. Think outside the box, and for most, that box is your physical location.

Time Horizon

Plan six months, one year, two years, and three years in advance. Never change the six-month plan. Review your financial reporting against that plan to determine how you did. Major deviations (positive or negative) must be assessed. Likewise, do not alter your one-year plan midstream.

If you blow your plan away, consider two things. First, take a moment and enjoy your operational success. Second, take another moment and lament your inability to properly articulate a plan. Running things right includes appropriate planning. Once you have a year of results to analyze, you can (and should) adjust your mid-range and long-term plans to accurately reflect your trajectory, progress, capital, and needs. Review your results monthly against your plan to determine operational patterns. These patterns will help you drive the organization rather than to blindly follow behind it.

CHAPTER TWELVE

Accountability and Accounting

THE BOARD OF DIRECTORS

Now that you have the vision, mission, and values statements (collectively, the "Statement"), the budget, the financials, and the marketing plan, someone needs to implement all of it (collectively, the "Plan"). Your board is the starting point. Remember the sequence. *Stakeholders* (those interested in the outcome) *incorporate* (form) *the organization.* They elect directors. Directors appoint officers. Officers run the organization and report to the board and stakeholders.

The first action is the election of a board. This is the most critical piece in the process of making the Statement a reality. Pick from the best talent available anywhere. Remove racial, ethnic, scriptural, economic, and even, in some instances, philosophical differences to form a board capable of sustaining your vision. If you need capital, bring on the best banker and investment manager you can find. If you need to put more people in the seats, find a marketing genius.

As we discussed before, fellowship with those of disparate skill sets will make your board the engine you need. The right board will hire or acquire the right officers (the "Officers").

Friends and family reflect the natural inclination of choice for most newly formed corporations. Resist this impulse! Understand your mission statement, both from an ecclesiastical and a business perspective, and surround yourself with highly qualified individuals who can, through education, experience, relationships, and past success, help guide you toward your objectives.

Board members need not be members of your organization. Likewise, members of your board need not be your friends. The seminal issues must remain the following: integrity, skill sets which complement your mission, a track record of proven success in areas you need to round out your organization, and sufficient time to devote to your mission.

How many board members are required? There is no legal maximum, and while there is no legal minimum, the prudent leader will insist upon a number of directors that reflects the vision. If growth is an objective, a larger, more sophisticated board with multiple growth-oriented skill sets within diverse directors may be appropriate.

The real answer is, again, start with the vision and tailor your operation around it. Put the right people on the board in whatever number suits the premise—don't merely fill seats to surround yourself with people who tell you what you want to hear. Find the right people, make just enough room for them, and leave enough flexibility in the Bylaws to afford you the opportunity to expand the size of the board as growth or change occurs.

Some boards compensate their directors. No distinction is drawn between for-profit and nonprofit boards when it comes to compensation packages, other than some for-profit board members get stock options, warrants, and other incentives not available in the nonprofit corporation context.

Attract the best, and if they are worth it, pay them. The strength of your board and their ability to function together will be one of the most significant benefits and agents of growth and change for your organization.

If the board meets resistance (which often happens if it is the result of a restructure or if it is "not the way it used to be done"), first applaud yourself for doing what must be done. Resistance usually means those who are losing power fear the change, those who fear the change are, as a result of some level of introspection, aware of their inadequacies, and either way, if the choices for the board were and remain correct, the results will define and speak for the decision and its appropriateness. Learn all you can, call the play, and have faith.

ACCOUNTABILITY

Committees

Divide your board into salient committees. Typical committees include the finance committee, a marketing committee, an audit committee, an investment committee and, if you have a capital project, a development committee. Committees can, and often should, include individuals who are not members of the board. Committee meetings typically occur, at a minimum, as frequently as board meetings. Often they meet more frequently than the board.

Following the fall of Enron and similar corporate debacles and ethical voids that have plagued corporate America in recent, greed-filled years, the nonprofit and nonpublic sectors of the economy, while not legally bound by the mandates of the Sarbanes-Oxley Act of 2002, are being scrutinized and judged, often in a court of law, by the standards it set and the law that is evolving daily as a result of its passage. As a result, particularly in the context of boards, consider the inclusion of a corporate governance committee, an investment policy statement for the investment committee, audited financial statements by a firm other than the one that prepares the annual financial statements, and periodic reviews of corporate and legal documentation, including Bylaws, shareholders' agreements, minutes, resolutions and the like (a legal audit). It is unlikely that the level of scrutiny will subside any time soon; and to the contrary, it appears that statutes previously designed solely for publicly traded companies will soon be governing the activities of private for-profit and nonprofit entities.

Meetings

Meet with your board at least once a month in the early stages of your organization's growth. If you can continue this frequency, do so. At a bare minimum, meet quarterly. While most states legislate annual meetings as a requirement, multiple reasons exist for a higher frequency of board meetings. They keep you informed, your board members stay engaged, thus allowing you to benefit from their broad experience, the officers of your organization remain more accountable, and alter ego claims (a legal charge that the entity and its stakeholders are really one) are reduced.

Create a reporting protocol that provides every board member with the salient financial and operational data far enough in advance to allow every board member to come to the meeting prepared. In that regard, circulate an agenda well in advance of the meeting. This will not only ensure an efficient meeting in light of the preparedness of the members, but it will allow the board members to add, if necessary, agenda items they believe are important for your organization.

The agenda should be specific, and each item should have an attendant time allocation. Allocate time for each topic, and save sufficient time for open discussion. Create discipline in your meetings, such that items are discussed and resolved within the time constraints set forth in the agenda. If a time allocation was deemed insufficient by a board member, they had, prior to the meeting, ample opportunity to say so. Appoint someone to enforce the time limitations reflected in the agenda.

The chairperson should and must control the meetings so the important business appropriately on the agenda can be adequately covered. If properly drafted, items not appropriately on the agenda in a timely fashion may not even be able to be acted upon due to insufficient notice pursuant to the mandate of the Bylaws.

Have all members of your board become familiar with Robert's Rules of Order, and consider placing it in the initial board package provided to each incoming member. In that regard, create a board package that reflects the expectations of the board regarding time commitments, conflicts of interest, and other requirements of board involvement. Ensure that prospective board members clearly understand the Statement and expectations before agreeing to join.

Accounting Rights

Your organization belongs and, as a statutory truism, is accountable to the members. As such, they are entitled to review the financial affairs of the organization. That said, their rights of review are a hybrid—they are vested in law and relegated or expanded in contract. Simply stated, the Bylaws determine the frequency of their accounting rights.

While this may vary from state to state, protect the functionality of your organization in the following ways: 1) Relegate accounting rights to normal business hours (usually defined as Monday through Friday between 9:00 A.M. to 5:00 P.M.); 2) Consider a biannual limitation or some other reasonable constraint; 3) Limit the amount of free copies; 4) Make the financial information available at the annual meeting of the members at the expense of the organization; and, 5) allow members or, alternatively, certified public accountants they hire, to copy information within prescribed times at their expense.

THE OFFICERS

The officers you need are president, secretary, and treasurer. Titles like chief executive officer, vice president, chief operating officer, church administrator, chief financial officer, etc. are not statutorily required. That said, design your organization to meet the needs reflected in your strategic plan. The day-to-day operations of your organization will be handled by the officers.

In a ministry organization context we recommend the benefits of a bifurcated (divided into two parts) board with the ecclesiastical leadership comprised of, in large measure, deacons or elders. While these titles vary among denominations, the concept is consistent. The organization is divided into the business and ecclesiastical segments. The plan has both.

Those portions of the plan that deal with money, endowment, legal issues, business development, and nonecclesiastical structure (some of which involves marketing and the monetization of products, services, and messages) are under the purview of the governing board and the officers, consultants, lawyers, and agents it hires.

The ecclesiastical segment of the organization, including ushers, the choir, auxiliaries, new members, prayer lines, etc. remain under the purview of the deacon board and those directed by the plan to accomplish the ecclesiastical agenda. Clearly there is cross-over as there should be. It is one organization; the operations fall within one plan, and ultimately, one leader stands before the people.

That said, even the leader of a faith-based organization has a board to answer to, the leader and the board answer to the congregation, and collectively, we answer to God. Let the answer not be we failed to efficiently administer the gifts and talents He gave us, for failing to rise to the level of our ability is wicked in the eyes of the Lord.

PRINCIPLES OF ACCOUNTING

Again, we strongly recommend fellowship and seeking out experts in fields that you may be unfamiliar with or feel that you need help understanding particular accounting terms and processes.

These are the basic functions of accounting:

- Assets.

- Liabilities.

- Revenue.

- Expenses.

- Earnings.

The basic accounting equation is: assets minus liabilities equals owner's equity. This agenda is reflected on the balance sheet and means, in plane English, *what you own minus what you owe equals what you are worth.* The balance sheet is a financial snapshot of your organization at a given time, usually at month end. Revenue minus expenses equals earnings and is presented on the *statement of operations* or income statement. The income statement shows the financial activity that occurs between balance sheets. In the *chart of accounts* you will define revenue streams and associated cost centers, costs for sales and marketing, general and administrative expenses, and designated funds. These topics are defined in more detail later in the chapter.

THE BALANCE SHEET

Again, assets minus liabilities equals owner's equity. These are the fundamental underpinnings of the balance sheet. The balance sheet simply reflects, at a given point in time, the viability of your organization financially. It does not evidence trends, reflect income, reflect expenses or anything other than how much you owned and what you owed on a given date.

As an operational tool, the balance sheet is more helpful to a banker than a leader. It is a historical document that a banker might insist upon to determine what assets exist to repay their loan. If, however, your income is trending down, your expenses are trending up, and your membership is dwindling, the banker may still make the loan. You just might not be able to pay it back. Let's look at the income statement to determine how to track operations.

THE INCOME STATEMENT

The income statement tells us how much revenue we took in, what we paid out, and what noncash expenses (depreciation of assets, etc.) were incurred. If our revenue is below our budget, our variance report (a report showing differences between our expectations and reality) would reflect the disparity and we could react accordingly. The same holds true with managing expenses. Regardless of whether expenses are recurring or nonrecurring, reporting them and managing them through the variance report and responses will ensure appropriate stewardship.

THE CHART OF ACCOUNTS

To understand your operation, we need to define the *income and expense streams*. Then, we need to categorize them in order to produce meaningful financial reports. These categories are called the *chart of accounts.*

- Do the expenses relate to the business or ecclesiastical functions of the church?

- Is the salary pastoral or related to security?

- Did you allocate a portion of the mortgage to the bookstore to determine independently how profitable the sale of products is? If you sell a book for $10 and it cost you $8, did you really make $2?

- What if you sold the same book to someone who heard you on the radio? Did you allocate a portion of the cost of radio to the sale?

COMPONENTS OF GOOD FINANCIAL STATEMENTS

Your financial statements should reflect your resources, historical data, (where have we been?), organizations with whom you work, consultants, your break-even analysis, where you have flexibility for spending, your growth (where you are going), restricted funds, overall review, and implementation of your vision.

SOURCES AND USES OF FUNDS

Where will your operational funds come from? Tithes and offerings? Grants? Ticket sales? Part of the analysis depends upon the expectation of the benefactors—are they expecting a tax deduction if they support your organization? The needs of the donors (the "Sources") are significant drivers in the formation process. How those funds will be used is another.

If the funds are to be used for investment purposes rather than to confer a public benefit, consider forming a for-profit entity. If the proceeds are intended to significantly benefit the founder or founders, likewise consider the formation of a for-profit entity. Remember, the formation documents and the Form 1023 you will be required to submit to the IRS will solicit answers to these questions, and receipt of your tax exempt designation will be dependent upon the appropriateness of these answers.

FINANCIAL REPORTING

Your financial reporting should, ultimately, include flash reports, monthly, quarterly, and yearly analysis, departmental reporting, government compliance, year-end tax reporting for members, management participation, and information systems reports. All of this reporting may seem daunting, but through fellowship, you will achieve appropriate reporting and visibility.

Nothing measured, nothing gained. The budget and business plan are worthless to you from an operational perspective if you can't track your performance against them in real time. How can you affect the outcome if you don't understand your performance?

If, however, you knew that your income increased based upon a particular thematic message, would that help you? What if people told their friends to join your church based on a change in your delivery? These "intangibles" can and should be reported along with numerical performance to assist you in leading and growing.

If you failed to account for the true cost of your revenue, you did not gain a true picture of your profitability. Losses are never made up in volume. You have a fiduciary duty to understand your organization's financial picture and manage it appropriately.

Prosperity is not an accident. It is a process. Let's start.

Break-even Analysis

At what income level does your organization break even? What are your profit margins? Most nonprofit organizations do not understand their margins. Don't follow those who don't, and make sure that when dealing with a fool that he is not similarly occupied. You can't manage what you don't understand. Make sure you know your margins by profit center so you can adjust as needed.

Your revenue less the cost of producing that revenue equals your gross profit. If you sold books, the sale minus the cost of producing the book would equal gross profit. Gross profit less all remaining expenses (allocated mortgage expense, advertising, marketing, salaries, insurance, etc.) equals net profit. If your organization is not profitable, determine why, adjust, and come out swinging. Your vision never changes. Change your implementation.

RESTRICTED FUNDS

Many nonprofit organizations have restricted funds. Examples include scholarship funds, building funds, and the like. These must remain segregated and can only be used for their stated purpose. Violating this mandate will give rise to a host of unpleasant circumstances discussed earlier. Never violate these sacrosanct rules.

SALIENT REPORTING

You should receive your numbers in a format that comports with your style. If you spoke English exclusively, you would not buy a book written in Spanish regardless of whether it was considered the best book ever written. Your financial reports are designed (or should be) as a management tool (other than giving reports and year-end audited reports). Use them accordingly.

THE FLASH REPORT

Demand and receive a weekly flash report telling you the key financial indicators of your organization. If you are a church, include the weekly message to determine whether it impacts the financial performance. If tithing is trending downward, address it. If your attendance has decreased (include a count weekly), evangelize outside the house. Know your income by service, the message, extraordinary giving and expenses, and the variance against the budget for all of these. Also know your cash position weekly. See Appendix for sample flash reports.

MONTHLY PROFIT AND LOSS REPORTS

Profit and loss reports, or income statements, should be reviewed monthly. These will contain the back-up detail not reflected in the flash reports. Make time monthly to spend with your finance department understanding any anomalies so you can track them against your budget intelligently. Your involvement will also protect against any potential inappropriate behavior.

GIVING REPORTS

Your donors are entitled to timely giving reports. If your financial reporting system is tight, this process will be automatic with very little effort. You also need to understand who your donors are so you can communicate with them appropriately. Remember, these reports are tools of communication with your donors, your life blood, and they must be timely, articulate, and accurate. They should also be accompanied by a letter from the leader.

Let your congregation understand your love, respect, and appreciation for all they do since weekly they evidence their love, respect, and appreciation for what you do. You have asked for a commitment from them of their decreasing free time and financial resources in an environment where your competition is ever increasing. With approximately 67,000 African-American, 150,000 Latino, and over 200,000 Caucasian churches in the United States alone (and over 1.2 billion Christians worldwide), your members have many choices other than you and your anointing. Show them the love.

CREDIT

Would you hire a chief financial officer whose credit would not allow him to obtain a service station charge card? If not, why should I worship at a church with bad credit or no credit? Churches can obtain credit outside the credit of its pastor. Again, seek fellowship regarding the creation, enhancement, and maintenance of your business credit profile. Better credit means lower interest rates, more opportunities, and the ability to lead by example.

Faith-based Investing

According to fund research firm Morningstar, the value of assets held by faith-based funds has jumped nearly sevenfold since 2000 to $15.9 billion (2006). Investors are finding that they don't have to sacrifice returns to invest with religious values in mind. The values closely watched by many religious funds overlap with good corporate governance principles, which may be behind their solid returns.

Community-based Investing

We all bear the responsibility to pursue and achieve a triple bottom line of social, financial, and environmental performance. Without prosperity, there is no philanthropy. This is a leadership principal that must be engaged in and demonstrated as the example rather than an option.

The *goals* of investing in the community are:

- Market rate returns on investment.

- Focus investment in underserved communities.

The *benefits* of community-based investing are:

- Job creation for the community.

- Wealth building.

- Affordable housing.

- Catalytic economic development in underserved communities.

- Sustainable design and construction.

TRIPLE BOTTOM LINE INVESTING

Here are some guidelines for triple bottom line investing:

An article in *ING Investment Management* magazine states that "...funds must be invested in companies that not only try to maximize shareholder value, but also focus on **stakeholder value**, with due respect for people, planet and profit, the sustainable triple bottom line."

Avoid companies that promote or produce products that are environmentally harmful (automobiles, mining), avoid companies that restrict human rights. Invest in "green" energy, products, and methods. Re-energizing the project site may reduce the number of homeless, needy, and drug addicts. Triple bottom line investing may help rehabilitate methadone addicts, provide job training and provide construction jobs that will rejuvenate your community.

Marshall Perry, a marketing expert and member of the Duraflame board of directors was struggling, along with fellow board members and officers, to penetrate a portion of the South deeply resistant to manufactured fire logs. While Duraflame, with a compelling market share in excess of 70 percent, could survive without gaining this segment, they understood their market, competition, and product well, and understood the need for an opportunity to grow. Ultimately, they created a log with significantly fewer pollutants than are released by traditional wood burning fires, and with similar (or better) heat and duration properties. Their environmental responsibility became the agent for change necessary to break into what was previously perceived as an impregnable market segment.

What Is Measured

Direct Impacts or Effects are the amount of total dollars spent and resulting indirect jobs created. Jobs can be measured in raw number of jobs or hours of labor. We utilize numbers of jobs.

Indirect Impacts or Effects are those economic effects which are the impacts upon other industries based on known multiplier effects for certain activities from the direct expenditures made.

Induced Impacts or Effects are the resulting household expenditures that result from the flow of money to individuals as measured in the direct and indirect impacts.

Financial Bottom Line

The financial bottom line for any investment remains significant. Market rate returns will attract private investment for the entity. Public subsidy and private investment combine to enhance impacts. Tax credits and other tools reduce project costs. Reduced costs can lead to reduced rents, enhanced services, higher quality construction, additional features and, sustainable (green) construction. These, in turn, have potential to create additional jobs and significant social benefits.

Social Bottom Line

There will be a social impact from your investments in the community. These include:

• Job creation (construction and operations).

- Imported funds reduce burden on local agencies, municipal funds.

- Funds stay in the community, recycle.

- Increased fiscal returns from new job support services.

- Restoration of historic structures.

- Support of arts and cultural organizations.

ENVIRONMENTAL BOTTOM LINE

Through wise planning, the investment can have the following environmental impacts:

Well lit schools and buildings have been shown to increase productivity, test scores, and financial results.

Natural ventilation reduces "sick building syndrome," reduces sick days, and increases productivity.

Reduced dependence on utilities reduces operations costs and pollution.

Reduced Volatile Organic Compounds (VOC) improves indoor air quality—(Americans are indoors 90 percent of the day).

Reduced impact on landfills, sewer systems, energy generation, CO_2 creation.

Simply stated, we have a responsibility to teach and preach the triple bottom line of investing and operating in order to stay strong and live long. What legacy will you be responsible for providing? Will it make you proud? Will your grandchildren drink clean water and breathe clean air?

Chapter Thirteen

Organizational Operations

These Principles Apply To Everyone

Your operations will transmute as you grow. If they are ill conceived and lack discipline and strategic planning at the gestation phase, they will devolve from bad to worse. Start right, stay right.

It is a fallacy that nonprofit organizations, faith-based or otherwise, are neither permitted nor designed to earn profit. As the shepherd of your faith-based nonprofit corporation (business or family), it remains both your calling and fiduciary duty to ensure the ongoing viability and profitability of your organization.

This segment of the text is designed to offer you grounded, straight talk advice on how to do just that. These same principals can and should be adopted by and adapted for all of you desirous of achieving financial independence and freedom.

Many faith-based nonprofit organizations engage in multiple business enterprises and activities. Some of those activities may, and often do, require resources from the nonprofit entity in order to grow. Issues of commingling often ensue if preventative measures and proper structuring are not followed. As such, multiple entities are often formed. While affiliated, these entities should be maintained separately. This section explores this concept in some depth and provides numerous suggestions.

This text is also intended to provide practical operational tips regarding subjects including: collection of tithes and offerings, security, fundraising, grant procurement, accounting for donors, financial reporting, lifestyle and the ecclesiastical perspective, forming and prospering in the television arena, radio, marketing, merchandising, obtaining corporate sponsorship for your church or business, and much more.

TITHES AND OFFERINGS

Most faith-based nonprofit organizations generate the substantial majority of their operating capital from tithes and offerings. Though budgeting and Scripture militate toward consistent tithing, more organizations rely upon offerings for sustenance. Unfortunately, offerings typically vary in amount more radically than tithes. As such, the following truism, coupled with the following principles, will afford your organization fertile ground to grow and prosper.

Teach tithing. Attempt to weight your income toward, at a minimum, 70 percent recurring, dependable revenue streams (including tithing, endowment residuals, fixed giving campaigns and the like) and less toward offerings. Without consistent cash flow, budgeting becomes undependable. Without dependable budgeting, leading your organization will remain analogous to a perilous attempt to navigate level five rapids on a rubber raft. You may find the shore fortuitously, by you may not like how you look or feel when you arrive.

We have never seen an organization achieve goals that we failed to set, and it is futile to set economic goals without consistent cash flow.

FUNDRAISING

An exhaustive explanation of alternate endowment and fundraising strategies is beyond the scope of this text, but suffice it to say it is abundantly clear that the landscape is highly competitive and the battle for offering dollars is fierce, especially in the United States where there are approximately 417,000 churches. That said, missioned giving is on the rise, endowment strategies ranging from life insurance, nonprofit debentures (bonds), residual income from business enterprises incubated within your walls, grant writing, and residual income from intelligent investing will set you and your organization apart from the pack.

Further, by extension, if you preach and teach prosperity, your congregation will follow, your members will enjoy and share in that growth on individual levels, and ultimately, you will create your own circular network designed to endow your organization through the increased tithing, giving, and support from the members you helped teach and grow. These are truly Spiritual Solutions for Financial Freedom.™

Hidden Diamonds. Do you capture your weekly messages? Do you have significant content within this shrinking market? Research reveals that tape and DVD sales will continue to decline in upcoming months and years. Will you be ready for the changes technology will force upon you?

Within five years, tape sales will be obsolete, CD and DVD sales will decline, and digital downloads will reign supreme. Imagine little to no additional cost associated with electronic storage of your most valuable asset—your intellectual property—and the ability to repurpose it worldwide, with no shipping expenses, for a fee. Now imagine if your messages are in English, opening up the rest of the faith-based world to your products by translating them, if only into Spanish (40 million Latinos reside in the United States today) and sell them domestically exclusively. Now, include Mexico, Central and South America.

Again, at little additional cost, you have exponentially increased your potential market, and you created nothing new. You simply licensed your product and repurposed it. Other hidden diamonds are discussed in the Special Projects paragraph to follow.

ACCOUNTING FOR DONORS

Envelopes. Donor envelopes should be maintained for a minimum of three years from receipt (five years is even better). Each name should be maintained in the entity's database and provided to your tax preparer. Since, in most instances, the envelopes are your main source of information required to prepare the appropriate tax forms for your members (and the maintenance and enhancement of your database), alphabetical storage with an organized maintenance and retrieval system will assist you when it comes time to prepare tax forms (and to market products and services to your database).

Tax Forms. Your giving reporting is sacrosanct, both from a public relations standpoint (consider it an opportunity to communicate with and thank your membership) and from a self-preservation standpoint. These records must, without fail, remain accurate and be distributed in a timely manner. If your envelope system is properly designed, your counting system integrated with your financial and giving reporting and redundancy put in place, the preparation of the giving reports will be perfunctory.

Most organizations merely send the sterile 990 reports to their members. Send a cover letter. Thank your members. Ask them to remain or become more engaged. Ensure that tangible signs of growth are reported, similar to annual reports in the secular world, when these reports are given to the members. Use the report to mark the giving floor, not the ceiling. The report itself should, if handled properly, become the least significant portion of this mailing. Effective communication at this critical juncture will reinforce the fact that the reflected number merely constitutes the number your member or members shall exceed in the coming year as your teachings settle in and your membership becomes more prosperous.

Special Projects. Always use segregated accounts for special projects, such as the building of a new school, the expansion of your sanctuary, or the acquisition of television equipment. As with all aspects of your organization, always budget each special project. Thereafter, set tangible, achievable (with a stretch) milestones, and report to the congregation on the success in achieving those milestones.

Also, recognize that, just like your organization is striving to achieve a legacy, so are your members. Allow them to purchase and donate a portion of the sanctuary, a chair, a brick, bench, plaque, or room. Your members own your organization. Never forget that, and by extension, afford them the glory of reminding the world. Also, consider an endowment strategy which gives your members the opportunity to honor their loved ones with the foregoing.

The segregated accounts are important from another perspective. Failing to adhere to this formality, particularly in the post Enron, Sarbanes Oxley climate, could lead to disastrous results. Remember, conservatism when dealing with the finances of a faith-based nonprofit remains a sacrosanct principal. Err on the side of caution always. A commingling determination by any tribunal would cause your organization and the culpable parties no end of pain.

1. Planned Giving. The life insurance tools and examples discussed shortly are excellent planned-giving instruments which leverage money and create exponential results. If your organization engages experts to assist members in their estate planning, other gifts can be appropriately made. A committee of the governing board should be formed to centralize planned giving, endowment and sponsorship activities for your organization so large donors are not being asked to sponsor a luncheon instead of your new Bible institute.

2. Endowment Strategies. Your music ministry is, at present, an expense item on your income statement. Does your church offer music lessons? Have you sought sponsorship or the gifting of new instruments or equipment from corporate donors desirous of reaching your target market?

By way of example, let's assume your annual music ministry budget, which includes expenses associated with worship service musicians, is $50,000. If you could obtain a $500,000 grant or other sponsorship from an instrument manufacturer, record company, or a foundation dedicated to the education of youth through music, your ministry would become perpetually endowed. Simply stated, conservatively invested, the endowment (probably restricted funds) would generate a return that could, forever, pay the salient expenses.

This has additional benefits. First, your church could now redirect the funds previously spent on this ministry toward other necessary causes, the reduction of debt, additional investments, or any other purpose which comports with the mission. Second, the endowment could be added to and generate cash flow to improve the program. Finally, though restricted, these funds improve your balance sheet and allow you to leverage your organization, if necessary, to achieve other goals.

3. Sponsorship. Review your income statement, and identify your largest creditors—those you spend the most money on annually. Have you ever asked them to become a sponsor rather than pay them money? Did you ever ask your insurance provider to sponsor your health fair? Why not?

For those of you on television, have you ever sold a commercial spot to a financial institution and asked them to sponsor your broadcast? Why not? Like-minded, faithful corporate citizens are scratching their heads trying to determine how to reach the people who come to see you without you asking. Don't you believe everyone involved would benefit if you facilitated the marriage?

City of Refuge Church had, on one broadcast, approximately ten commercial spots per week at its disposal to use as it saw fit. Initially, conventional wisdom (and the following of the herd mentality) led to the use of these spots exclusively for the sale of the church's products and the edification of the viewers regarding calendar events. Suffice it to say these valuable tools were being misapplied.

Today those same spots have created a revenue stream and reciprocal promotional opportunities that, in real dollars, have created revenue sufficient to allow the church to air its broadcast on additional networks at a minimal additional out-of-pocket expense. The additional product sales and relationships gained by approaching the opportunity from a different angle far outweigh any incremental sales that could have been achieved by taking the traditional approach.

RESPONSIBLE INVESTING

Faith-based nonprofit organizations should heavily weigh their investment portfolios toward a zero net loss of capital type investment vehicles. Faith-based leaders must remain extremely conservative in their investment strategies as the shepherds of their congregations' resources. As entities devoid of exposure to taxation (barring cataclysmic circumstances as discussed below), tax free investment vehicles usually serve little purpose for the organization (though the same is not true for the leaders and members). Market dependent, government backed instruments, Moody's AAA-rated debt instruments, AAA-rated Blue Chip index paper, Blue Chip equities and related, and relatively secure investments (including sufficient liquidity) with a threshold goal of outpacing inflation are the underpinnings of a responsible, conservative portfolio. Depending on the size and viability of your organization, real estate, particularly income-producing real estate, may likewise suit your long-term financial goals and needs.

Remember, however, that real estate is usually a long-term investment with little or no short-term liquidity. Tailor your investment plan toward your short (six months to one year) and long-term (three to five year) objectives.

Interview multiple investment advisors. Task the board, and more specifically the finance and investment committees, with the job of interviewing and recommending a minimum of three suitable advisors. References should be checked, background searches are appropriate (and the refusal to submit to same should raise a red flag that should not be lowered), and the faith-based nonprofit leader should choose from three such individuals universally recommended by the board. Then, ensure that the advisor helps the investment committee craft an investment policy statement the board ratifies and the church adheres to.

Invest first in your core business. Practically speaking, your faith-based nonprofit organization is a business, and like any business, a product is produced and delivered, a physical plant is required to deliver it, marketing is required to increase demand, and customer demand is met through a channel of distribution.

Investing in yourself means having adequate space to comfortably seat your congregation and obtaining sufficient land to adequately park your congregants' vehicles. Depending on your particular stage of existence, you may also have to invest in a bow truss or other high ceiling to enable adequate lighting, sound and television equipment, and CD/DVD burners for your sermons. Editing and similar equipment may also be necessary.

Believe it or not, again, like any secular business, your products, even the sermons on Sunday, bear an economic cost. Once you set up your financial reporting and tracking properly, you will be able to ascertain it with specificity. Each additional chair will generate additional revenue when you operate optimally. Investments in marketing should, properly spent, translate into a broader based ministry which, in turn, should translate into product revenue, honorariums, and fellowship elsewhere which, again, translates into the foregoing.

Apply the "inside out" principle. Invest inside your house first. Then, use surplus capital to invest outside with the goal of beginning to fund an endowment sufficient to sustain your organization if, for whatever reason, you were unable to deliver the message on Sunday. Leverage your fixed assets to create alternative sources of revenue.

A wonderful example is the Getty Trust. J. Paul Getty issued a directive that his heirs and those entrusted with his estate could never charge the public to view his art collection. Couple this with the fact that the Getty Museum in Los Angeles, California, cost the Trust over $1 billion to develop and, at a minimum, 5 percent of the Trust must be distributed annually. To the layperson, this directive painted a grim picture.

Through extremely prudent investing, the Getty Trust has grown over 1,000 percent and presently exceeds $11 billion. As a comedic postscript, Mr. Getty forgot to proscribe his heirs and trustees from charging the public to park prior to viewing his art. That has proven to be a major profit center.

Turning this wisdom toward your organization, invest your surplus resources prudently, follow sage advice, diversify, seek alternative sources of revenue beyond tithes and offerings and strive for endowment status, such that the earnings on your portfolio cover your operating costs and beyond. This is how legacies are born. It's your turn.

KEY PERSON LIFE INSURANCE

Leaders seek knowledge. That is why you bought this book. Leaders care for their organization and its members. Responsible shepherds care for their flocks, now and in the future. What happens to your organization (your church, company, or family) when something happens to you? Key person life insurance strategies answer this question. Insure to ensure. A policy on your life must be a policy by which you live. The premiums are usually affordable, and the finance committee of your board (or you personally) should seek the best resources available to advise you based on your organization and its specific needs and goals. These policies can and should grow with you.

FIDELITY INSURANCE

Your organization survives, in large measure, on the after-tax, hard-earned money given to it on the faith of those whose trust you have sworn, through scriptural, secular, and common law, to protect. Likewise, insurance exists to assist you in doing so. Ask your insurance agent about fidelity insurance. Make sure everyone who comes into contact with funds in your organization is identified to your agent and referenced in the policy. Likewise, ensure that you have the full legal name, address, driver's license, passport, telephone numbers and numbers of relatives of all who are in the employ of your organization, all who count its money, and all who provide intimate services on its behalf, like financial consultants. These concepts will be covered in more detail in the Risk Management section. In later chapters, written agreements like non-disclosure, noncompetition, noncircumvention, nonsolicitation and nondisparagement agreements will likewise be discussed.

SECURITY

As the shepherd of your entity and the members it serves, the assets you are entrusted to protect must remain secure. This responsibility shall forever remain sacrosanct, and the absence of that security has, on many occasions, brought down the faithful and powerful, regardless of culpability. Often the *appearance* of impropriety *transcends proof* to the contrary. Nationally, many faith-based nonprofits use their deacons, elders, members, or others to count and account for tithes and offerings. Often those funds are in cash. Multiple levels of security should be observed.

Cameras. Conspicuous and inconspicuous monitoring equipment may be a good idea. This equipment should be installed by security professionals not in any way involved with either the ecclesiastical or governing boards. Further, if your organization's culture militates toward allowing members to count tithes, offerings, and other seeds or income, non-members should be among their ranks.

The counting room must be secure, and protocols should be established for those entering and leaving. Purses, backpacks, and other items, including overcoats, robes, and the like should not be allowed in the counting room. Those included in the counting process should be provided with documentation to sign which expressly authorizes random searches of their person and bags by security. Redundancy in the system of counting and recounting should be strictly enforced.

It is suggested that, if you do not presently have surveillance equipment, you install it without the knowledge of those presently counting the money. If nothing is revealed, you remain truly blessed. If something is revealed, you remain truly blessed by the Lord's provision of an opportunity to excise a tumor from your organization before it metastasizes.

Armored Transport. Many organizations out-source the counting and depositing functions, and many viable, credible companies exist for this purpose. These entities carry their own insurance (including fidelity insurance) and are extremely proficient at counting and accounting for the money. You and your board should consider this function seriously, weigh the cost versus the benefits, and make a choice tailored toward the culture, size, and objectives of your organization.

Security for You and Your Congregation. Security personnel can and should perform a multitude of tasks, including but not limited to guarding the counting room; conducting random searches of those charged with the responsibility of counting the organization's money; guarding the leaders, elders, members, and property of the organization; directing traffic; guarding inventory and equipment; and creating a safe, calm environment within which your organization can flourish. Unbeknownst to many, properly framed and presented, certain aspects of your insurance may likewise be reduced.

Opponents of security may argue that accessibility to the leader will be hindered and the organization's exposure will increase due to potential clashes with security. In response, the authors humbly suggest that the leader should be afforded the inalienable right to some freedom and privacy, and since the primary function of security is to observe, report, and deter through mere presence, altercations will and empirically are largely prevented.

Finally, outside security personnel should be required to carry their own liability and worker's compensation insurance in most jurisdictions, and you should ensure that your organization is a named insured on a comprehensive liability policy with sufficient per occurrence and aggregate insurance limits to protect the present and expected near-term asset base of the organization.

On the Road. As your ministry grows, and with it your popularity, notoriety, and exposure, security becomes a bigger issue. This becomes even more critical if you are on television.

Have at least one person with you to observe, and if necessary, report all activity. This observer may become a critical witness to the occurrence or nonoccurrence of events which bring your conduct into question. An eyewitness to the propriety of your conduct may be all that protects your reputation and that of your ministry from someone who desires to harm you, profit, or otherwise benefit from you, or both. Having met the multiple wives of single leaders and the long lost parents of orphans who, on more occasions than you could imagine, are "only seeking what is rightfully theirs," heed the advice of the authors here. Your safety is of paramount importance. So is your reputation. Like a bad day, if you disagree, try saving any souls without one.

At Home. Never list your telephone number. Do not share your number with other than a coveted few. Have more than one e-mail address. Never have your mail delivered to your home. Take title to your home in the name of an entity, and use your counsel as the addressee on any publicly recorded documentation, including deeds, articles of incorporation or organization, phone bills, etc.

Are you paranoid if they really are following you? Joking aside, you hold the key to unfettered interaction with others. Keep the key in your pocket. If you want to socialize, do so. But, protect your privacy and safety and that of those you love. Further, as a responsible steward of your organization, protecting yourself protects the ongoing viability of your organization.

INTERPLAY WITH FOR-PROFIT ENTITIES AND VENTURES

The faith-based nonprofit in the 21st century has become far more complex with, in many instances, multiple income streams, numerous diverse ventures, several entities, boards, officers, members, and beneficiaries. If strict adherence to the corporate formality of these distinct entities is ignored, a draconian, cataclysmic event can occur.

Imagine being the pastor of a church which has been in existence as a nonprofit religious corporation in good standing for 100 years prior to you taking over. You, as the ambitious, faithful, enterprising young pastor are anxious to avail your membership to sustainable growth of the congregation and its resources. You build a television and radio ministry, you sell books and tapes, and soon, you become a household name. Everyone from your boards to your congregation applaud your efforts and the results.

Your secretary, on the church payroll, likewise appreciates the ability to work for a person of faith in a growing ministry. He works from your home often and even assists you in collecting the rent from that eight-unit apartment complex you own and from which you tithe 10 percent to the church.

Though this example will appear extreme to you, the enemy lurks in all shadows. Using your secretary to collect the rent could, in the worst case scenario, afford the IRS the ammunition to attempt to rescind the nonprofit status of your organization. You are guilty of using church assets for personal gain. Taken to the extreme, if the nonprofit status is rescinded, the organization could be asked to pay taxes on all of the income derived from the inception of its charter, thus rendering an extremely viable organization insolvent.

PLANNING

Start with a well-defined organizational chart. Though neither dispositive nor exhaustive, remember, in any corporate structure, the members elect the board of directors, the board hires the officers, and the officers run the day-to-day operations of the organization.

Organization Flow Chart

Below is an example template for setting up your organization whether it is headed by a senior pastor or a CEO.

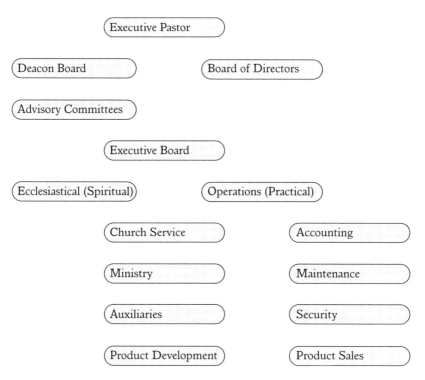

While oversimplified, this chart outlines clear channels of responsibility and accountability. People often fail ill-defined tasks; and responsibility without accountability will lead the leader toward unmet expectations. In that paradigm, the fault will rest solely with you.

Your statement will help you revise the lower, operational portions of your organizational chart. An excellent statement that is clearly reflected in a well-managed organization is: "We believe that the right people, given the right resources and freedom can achieve greatness."

The Homer T. Hayward Lumber Company, established in 1919, has transformed its mission statement into reality, and Hayward Lumber now boasts of sales in excess of $150 million annually, having achieved its most profitable year in its 86-year history in 2005.

Now, in a changing economy, while competitors perish, Hayward is prepared and poised to weather the storm and avail itself of opportunities unique to a declining sector and economy respectively.

In the nonprofit world, the City of Refuge's mission statement reflects the *Vision of Bishop Noel Jones*: "Reconciling people back to one another, to themselves, and to God." Following these vision principles, Bishop Jones has led the City from insolvency with less than 1,000 members in 1992 to a multimillion-dollar-a-year international ministry with over 15,000 members locally and hundreds of thousands of partners and followers worldwide. Remember, it starts with faith, a vision, and the discipline to carry it out.

Then, you need a plan.

BUSINESS PLAN

There are multiple facets of the business plan for any organization. For the purposes of this text and simplicity, we will separate them into two categories—the vision and the means. *The vision* identifies and details your goals, and *the means* defines the financial resources necessary to accomplish them. The order is intentional. The vision and goals should be broken into short, medium, and long-term periods of time. Examples could include increases in membership, increases in income, and missionary success. Your goals are and shall remain tailored to your organization and its mission. Accomplishing them will, in all instances, require means.

Your chief financial officer and the finance committee of your board should be tasked with the responsibility of creating the budget to be followed in meeting your goals and tracking your success (or lack thereof). Likewise, your finance department should prepare a variance report detailing the degree by which your organization missed the financial goals in either direction. You, as the leader, may also request a departmental narrative variance report on the nonmonetary goals that were either exceeded or against which your organization fell short.

Once your vision, goals, and budget meet, you are ready to define specific deliverables and the individuals tasked with their accomplishment. If you finish there, however, again, you will fail. It is critically important to likewise assign a timetable within which each task/objective must be met. Once that and the foregoing steps have been performed, you have the basics of a plan which can be tailored to meet the culture of your organization.

WORKING THE PLAN

Do not adjust the plan monthly. Review it quarterly. If your variance reports show that your basic assumptions were glaringly incorrect for an entire quarter, adjust the plan. Review and revise the plan annually if needed. Insure that each division/auxiliary prepares its own budget and plan, and incorporate them into the master plan of your organization. Ensure that your leaders buy into the plan. If they create and manage against the plans they create, they will. If you force feed them your goals, they will not. If you believe you must follow the latter strategy, you have the wrong leaders or you are the wrong leader. Either way, change now! Responsibility to stewardship requires it. Also, it is far easier to hold people responsible for failing to meet goals they set. As their leader, help ensure that their goals are realistic and not fabricated or stretched to please you.

ECONOMIC DEVELOPMENT CORPORATIONS

Economic Development Corporations (EDC) and Community Development Corporations (CDC) are variations of nonprofit entities typically formed to serve need-based missions within the communities in which they are formed. Generally, though not exclusively, they are formed for mission-based enterprise and real estate investing, respectively. Multiple forms of local, state, and federal funding exist for these entities, and in light of the existence of the Establishment Clause within the First Amendment to the United States Constitution, these nondenominational, secular nonprofit entities can, in many instances, avail themselves of funding not otherwise available to religious corporations.

Some examples include tax exempt bond financing, low income housing tax credits (LIHTC), multiple forms of grants, and much, much more. While a clear delineation must be maintained between your CDC/EDC and your other nonprofit and/or for-profit entities, these entities can share and assist you in advancing your entities' vision and mission. To be successful, however, and to avoid the appearance of impropriety or claim and exposure to alter-ego liability, separate boards, officers, directors, bank accounts, offices, budgets, and reporting must be maintained. Also, we strongly suggest that you consider avoiding the role of chairperson of the board of any entity you lead. Properly structured, this will not dilute your power, and further, the "cover" shall provide insulation and even guidance if your chairperson(s) is chosen wisely.

Remember, your fate rests with the mandate of the Bylaws, your effectiveness in the eyes of your constituency, and methodical planning and implementation in conformity with the guidance set forth herein. God will handle the rest.

FOR-PROFIT ENTITIES

Pay taxes! Strange advice from nonprofit authors and advisors, but in the wake of increasing and intensifying scrutiny, the tax exempt status of your organization, a most coveted asset, will be placed at risk if you fail to carefully heed this advice.

Modern ministry is a business, and a substantial one at that. It also now entails complex, multitiered business enterprises, divisions, and profit centers. Organize those thematically, and consider the formation of for-profit, tax paying entities with which to engage in certain activities. This should not be misconstrued to lead to the false dilemma respecting nonprofits earning a profit. As stated previously, the Getty Trust has a reserve in excess of $11 billion and is growing daily. The Gates Foundation, now combined with the "spill over" assets of Warren Buffet's estate, far exceed that amount. That said, if you preach outside your pulpit and receive honorariums, do so in a for-profit entity. We likewise advise the formation and use of for-profit entities for royalties from all forms of intellectual property.

Maximum Utility. Leverage your fixed assets to the extent possible without incurring unreasonable debt. By way of a previous example, how many days does your church hold services? What is being done with the sanctuary during the balance of the week? Can it be rented out? If not, can it serve as a community center? If the people come, chances are they will return to attend a service.

Does your church have extra space? Does the community need child care? Parents go to where their children are cared for and safe. Based on what daycare costs, wouldn't it be better for working parents to pay those funds to your church? You then create a relationship between the parents and your faith-based nonprofit organization because they have developed trust through witnessing the proper care being taken of their children. There may be many other obvious opportunities that you and your church leadership ignored because "it wasn't done that way in the past." Welcome to 21st century church.

Bethany Square. City of Refuge outgrew its prior church property which is located in South Central Los Angeles. That property had very little debt and, although functionally obsolete for its previous use as a facility for the City of Refuge during its growth, could be redeveloped to serve the community and advance the interests of the church. (See www.bethanysquare.com.)

The board determined that a sale was appropriate, and an offer was presented. Bishop Jones felt the church could not only sell the property but also participate in its development, and consequently, a higher offer was presented by an entity in which the authors have an interest. The offer included a carried 10 percent equity interest for the church and a carried 5 percent equity interest for Greater Bethany Economic Development Corporation, the EDC formed by Bishop Jones' predecessor, Bishop MacMurray.

When the offer was accepted, the property was leased to a Latino church, Iglesia de Cristo, and the commercial portion of the property, in line with the vision for the planned development, was leased to an adult daycare center. Alone, these two leases provided the church $22,000 per month it did not earn previously.

Thereafter, the purchase entity applied for and received an award of New Markets Tax Credits in the amount of $11 million. The funds generated from these tax credits paid for the predevelopment expenses, and now, the buyer is improving the formerly blighted neighborhood by developing approximately 155 for-sale, workforce condominiums, approximately 104 low income senior housing units above the adult daycare and approximately 40,000 square feet of commercial space, including a bank, child care center and a business incubator.

Environmentally sustainable materials and systems are also being employed so that the project, built green, can achieve Silver LEED Certification. This triple bottom line approach to investing and developing is in keeping with the mission of the church, the City of Los Angeles, the required profit motive (remember, there is no philanthropy without prosperity), and the environmental responsibility we all should feel. This project stands as proof that doing it right can be very profitable in all senses of that term.

Finally, again, consider the formation of those entities, be it corporations, Subchapter S or C, limited liability companies, limited partnerships or otherwise, thematically based on the nature of the intended income stream: Entertainment = Entity 1, books, tapes and DVDs = Entity 2, and Honorariums = Entity 3, etc.

Also, consult a specialized, trusted, referred CPA, lawyer, and consultants prior to forming all or any of these entities. Some funding sources, including certain angel investor funds (business "angels" are high net worth individual investors who seek high returns through private investments in start-up companies), target missioned investments with their investment dollars. Examples include nonprofit organizations, educational investments, and similar targets whose missions advance social causes.

The triple bottom line transcends socially responsible investing and addresses the environment as well. Alternative energy systems such as solar power, water consumption reduction devices like low-flush toilets, water cisterns designed to trap rain water and recycle it for irrigation uses, and building orientation techniques employed to maximize the sun's energy are examples of environmentally missioned investment opportunities, particularly when coupled by federal and state energy tax credits and similar incentives.

There can be no philanthropy without some level of prosperity. The third leg on the tripod of triple bottom line investing is the economic one. Positive change seldom happens without an economic incentive. Alternative energy systems that cost too much and fail to yield profit will not be well accepted by real estate developers as an example. Further, even the most socially responsible investments will ultimately be devoid of resources if a holistic approach that includes economic sustainability is not incorporated into the matrix.

If you liken it to a sailboat, the social calling is the navigation system, the environment is the weather, and the economics form the sail. Each item is integrated, and maximum efficiency is achieved only in harmony. Fail to respect the weather and the tiny ship is lost. Try to achieve the mission on the high seas without the sail. Even a sunny day won't save you in the middle of the ocean without navigation tools. The triple bottom line, once embraced in its entirety, like the trilogy, is the truth of the modern day investment world (and the undisclosed truth of the past, present, and future).

THE BUSINESS INCUBATOR

Modern ministry can no longer survive on tithes and offerings alone. That diminishing returns concept extends to all nonprofit entities. Consider as a partial solution, the case of New York University (NYU) School of Law and the New York Bagel Company. In the early years, NYU Law School was a fledgling, in need of funding, growth, and prestige; it was dwarfed in all material respects by its rival, Columbia University. A very aggressive and progressive decision was made by the board of trustees to invest in a small business, the New York Bagel Company. That investment turned into a multimillion dollar endowment which allowed NYU Law School to compete, flourish, and become one of the leading law schools in the nation. That can likewise happen to you.

If you invest in your stakeholders, they will invest in you. Imagine investing in five of your members' businesses through a variety of means, including allowing them to use your facility for little or no rent, lending them the periodic advice of the investment committee of your board to assist them in their businesses, or offering infrastructure support, like using your switchboard to help a member provide customer service.

Now, imagine that you offered this help in exchange for 10 percent of each of the three businesses you provided assistance to and they proved successful. First, your church would reap the benefits of your members' success. Second, more members could and probably would, if coached by you, become employed. Third, you would, in all likelihood, attract new members. Fourth, additional success within your membership has a linear relationship to your success overall. Finally, the equity in these businesses would be an asset on your church's balance sheet and could result in the benefit of an endowment.

This circle of success is beyond dispute. Try it. In addition to asking for a percentage of the businesses of those your church assists, have each board member of each company you help bring one new member to church a month. Do the math.

Church Risk Management

Simply stated, risk management is recognizing the threats for law suits and insurance issues and doing everything possible, *within reason,* to eliminate these threats, reduce their frequency or mitigate their potential damage to your organization. There is a rise in the number of claims and lawsuits against churches, leaders, and religious organizations. The common response to any accusation is denial, minimization, and/or blame. The church must take every accusation seriously and responsibly. Again, remember fellowship, and consult trusted advisors to help guide you from formation through insurance and beyond.

INSURANCE

Following proper formation and the strict adherence to corporate formalities, the next step in risk management is proper insurance coverage. Insurance is the transfer of risk from the church to the insurance company. The church is paying a fee in exchange for the assumption of liability by a third party. Find an insurance company with extensive experience insuring churches. Put the right people in the right seats on your bus.

Though clearly not exhaustive, main areas of protection that you will need insurance for include: property liability, general liability, sexual misconduct liability, directors' and officers' liability, employment practices liability, medical payments, and workers compensation. You might want to consider adding coverage for wrongful acts by worship leaders, officers, trustees, business administrators, and pastors. You may also consider tail coverage and umbrella coverage.

EMPLOYMENT PRACTICES

Employment practices liability (EPL) insurance covers a religious institution in areas relating to employment including discrimination, wrongful termination, and sexual harassment.

This is especially important as the number of employees increases and if the church has a school or daycare ministry.

AVOIDING LITIGATION

You should likewise, at a minimum, have a: child protection policy, transportation policy, property policy, responding to emergencies and crises policy, workers compensation and playground safety policy.

Ministries. When you add new people to your staff, make sure to add their names to your policy. Send a description to your agent. Remember that the church can be named in any law suit—so can the directors, officers, pastors, and others.

IMPORTANT THINGS TO REMEMBER

The church is responsible for anything that goes on at a church-sponsored activity and at a church owned/controlled location. The church and the church board are responsible for any event in the church and on its property. Implement policies and procedures for activities on and off church property, have them vetted by your advisors and agent, and follow them. If something occurs that is perceived as a liability by those in charge, tender a claim, in writing. Make sure that everyone working and/or volunteering knows the protocols regarding claims, insurance, service of process, and important documents.

LITIGATION

If there is a claim against the church here are some helpful hints:

- Document everything.

- Remember, you are a church. Don't be afraid to minister to those who may have been harmed while in your care. That said, likewise consult your advisors immediately.

- Have one person handle the claim in accordance with your policies and procedures.

RESPONDING TO EMERGENCIES AND CRISES

It is important that the church has a plan in place in case of emergencies such as fire, medical, or natural disasters. This plan should be posted, distributed, included in the employee handbook and/or policies and procedures manual and practices to ensure that it can be followed efficiently and safely.

CHAPTER FOURTEEN

Cautions and Common Mistakes

As in any venture in life, be it business, personal, social, educational, or financial, there are as many risks as there are benefits. Being aware of the possible risks allows you to avoid them or at the least, soften the blow. A few cautions and common mistakes are detailed for you in this chapter to provide you with knowledge and empower you with the confidence you need to reach your goals.

Some of the topics in this chapter have been touched upon previously but these are important enough to review again, as much depends on establishing and maintaining your personal and organizational footing on solid legal ground.

OVERCOMPENSATION

Intermediate sanctions under the Internal Revenue Code (IRC) impose a penalty of up to 200 percent on the recipient of overcompensation and a penalty of up to 10 percent on a manager who approves the payment. (See IRC 4958.) These sanctions apply to public benefit and religious corporations but may not apply to mutual benefit corporations.

Thus, when an officer is also a director, any board action to approve the officer's compensation should contemplate the rules on self-dealing transactions and on transactions in which a director has a financial interest.

PASTORAL COMPENSATION

Form an independent compensation committee populated with CPAs, compensation experts, and others with no ongoing connection to your nonprofit organization. Have them survey relevant organizations in your location to determine what similar officers are paid. Have them determine the ceiling for your compensation. Make sure your compensation is well below the ceiling, and even consider a number below their recommendation.

Shift as much of your compensation to the for-profit organization as you can reasonably without endangering its viability. The result will be a shifting of the burden of proof to the IRS to determine, by a preponderance of the evidence, that your compensation is unreasonable. Their burden will be extremely difficult if you follow this procedure and fortify it with an employment agreement reflecting the appropriate compensation, particularly after that agreement is ratified by your board.

This ratification provides you two additional layers of insulation—the Business Judgment Rule (the standard that governs the behavior of board members and officers in conjunction with the organizations they shepherd), and D and O Insurance (Directors and Officers Insurance).

FIDUCIARY OBLIGATIONS AND RULES

The term *fiduciary* refers to anyone who holds a position requiring "trust, confidence, and scrupulous exercise of good faith and candor. It includes anyone who has a duty, created by a particular undertaking, to act primarily for the benefit of others in matters connected with the undertaking. A fiduciary relationship is one in which one person reposes trust and confidence in another person, who 'must exercise a corresponding degree of fairness and good faith.'" (Black's Law Dictionary, 7th edition, 1999). The type of persons who are commonly referred to as fiduciaries will include the corporate directors.

A nonprofit director's fiduciary duties include the duty of care, the duty of inquiry, the duty of loyalty, and the duty to comply with investment standards. Like directors of for-profit corporations, directors of nonprofit corporations owe a fiduciary duty to the corporation they serve and to its members, if any.

The assets of a nonprofit charitable organization are deemed held in charitable trust. The charity's directors must conduct the corporation's affairs in a manner consistent with the purposes for which it was formed. If the directors fail to comply with the rules governing the charitable trusts in which the assets are held, or if they operate the organization in a manner that departs from its stated charitable purposes, they can be held accountable.

Examples include directors of a corporation, a lawyer vis a vis her clients and a therapist. The director has a duty of care, inquiry, loyalty, and competence. Since the assets of a nonprofit are deemed, as a matter of law, to be held in a charitable trust for the beneficiaries (Church = members), the directors must conduct the corporations' affairs in a manner consistent with the purposes for church the entity was formed. Failure to adhere to these fiduciary duties can and will expose the directors. Intentional failure to do so may also vitiate (reduce value or impair quality) the protections provided by D and O Insurance.

BUSINESS JUDGMENT RULE

The standard the courts apply in deciding whether a director, acting without a financial interest in the decision, satisfied the requirements of careful conduct imposed by the law is called the business judgment rule. The business judgment rule applies *only* if the director has no interest in the subject matter on which business judgment is being exercised.

DUTY OF LOYALTY

A director must act in a manner that the director believes to be in the best interests of the corporation and all of its members, including the members of minority factions, and to administer their corporate powers for the common benefit (the "duty of loyalty").

OPPORTUNITIES

If a director becomes aware of an opportunity or a transaction that would be of interest or benefit to the corporation, the director must disclose the opportunity to the corporation and permit it to take advantage of the opportunity, if it so desires. Failure to do so is called "usurpation of a corporate opportunity," and is typically not an action covered by insurance and exposes the director or directors.

LOAN TRANSACTIONS

A religious corporation is not prohibited from making loans to, or guaranteeing obligations of, its directors or officers. The liability of directors who approve such loans or guaranties is governed by the general standard of care requirements for ordinary transactions.

There will be no personal negligence liability if the nonprofit is insured and there is no finding of willful misconduct or gross negligence by a tribunal of competent jurisdiction.

SALE, EXCHANGE, OR LEASE OF PROPERTY

As long as the foundation or other nonprofit entity does not pay rent directly or indirectly to a disqualified person, such use of property is permitted. If the disqualified person's property is subject to debt, the private foundation may not assume the debt.

The sale, exchange, or lease of property between a private foundation and a disqualified person is self-dealing. The self-dealing ban does not apply to a disqualified person's donation of property to a private foundation.

EXTENSION OF CREDIT

Self-dealing includes lending money or extending credit between a private foundation and a disqualified person. Self-dealing includes furnishing goods, services, or facilities between a private foundation and a disqualified person.

PENALTIES FOR VIOLATING RULES AGAINST SELF-DEALING

The IRS automatically imposes an annual penalty tax on the self-dealing action equal to 5 percent of the amount involved. An annual penalty tax of 2.5 percent of the amount involved (up to a maximum tax of $10,000 for each act of self-dealing) may also be imposed on a foundation manager who knowingly participated in a self-dealing transaction, unless it was not willful and was for reasonable cause. (See IRC 4941.) The manager has a complete defense if he or she acted in reliance on the advice of counsel, expressed in a reasoned legal opinion. (See Reg. 53.4941(a)-1(b)(6).)

ADDITIONAL CONFLICT-OF-INTEREST REGULATIONS

Conflicts could also exist if a director is a realtor or contractor confronted with such issues as the regulation of commercial signs or the use of particular construction products or materials that do not involve a material financial interest.

Many nonprofit corporations want directors to disclose conflicts that may influence their corporate decisions, even if no material financial interest is involved.

PUBLIC CHARITY CLASSIFICATION

Can an IRC 501(c)(3) organization qualify for Public Charity Classification under IRC 509(a)? To determine the answer you have to ask the following questions:

- Will the primary activity be that of a church, school, hospital, or medical research organization operating in conjunction with a hospital?

- If not, will the primary source(s) of support be from: contributions from the founder and his or her relatives?

- Will contributions come from a large number of unrelated people?

- Will gross receipts come from the operation of an exempt activity?

Note: IRC 509(a) divides IRC 501(c)(3) organizations into private foundations and other types of organizations, usually known as public charities. Fairly onerous provisions designed to prevent abuse are applied to private foundations.

A major issue of concern is the deductibility of contributions made before obtaining determinations. Normally, the determination on a timely filed application will be retroactive to the date of organization. If for some reason, however, it is not retroactive, is not obtained, or is a different determination from the one expected, the question arises how prior contributions will be categorized.

Concerning its own income tax liability, the entity will either be taxable or nontaxable, depending on the outcome of the determination.

Tax exempt corporations obtain funds from several sources, such as charitable contributions, membership fees, and similar assessments; auctions, dinner dances, athletic events, and other fundraising efforts; borrowing; business activities; and investments. Subject to some exceptions, a tax exempt corporation may generally carry on business and investment activities itself or through other entities.

In some circumstances, income derived from sources other than charitable contributions and borrowing will be taxed as unrelated business taxable income. In a few situations, a tax exempt corporation's ownership interest in another entity can affect the income tax liabilities of that entity or other entities. Income that is characterized as recapture of certain prior tax deductions will be taxed to an exempt organization.

A nonprofit organization otherwise exempt from federal income tax is taxed on net income realized from a regularly conducted trade or business that is unrelated to the purpose or functions that qualify the organization for tax exemption. Taxes may also be imposed on income from property subject to a mortgage or other encumbrance and assets purchased with borrowed funds, payments received from controlled entities, deemed distributions from insurance income of a controlled foreign corporation, and net income earned on certain private-use property funded with proceeds from tax exempt bond financing.

CAUTION!

If an organization's unrelated trade or business is or will be substantial, the organization may lose, or fail to obtain, tax exempt status. Unrelated business income could also result in a partial or complete loss of the welfare exemption from property tax, disqualification of tax exempt bond financing, and limitation on reduced postal rates.

CAUTION!

Unrelated Enterprise. An "unrelated trade or business" is an enterprise that is regularly carried on by an exempt organization and that is not substantially related (other than through the production of funds) to the organization's exercise or performance of its exempt purposes. IRC 513(a). Fundraising activities that are regularly carried on, including but not limited to, awards of premiums in consideration for charitable contributions, lotteries and golf tournaments will be unrelated businesses unless they are covered by a limited exclusion.

Unrelated Enterprise Rules. Be expansive in the articulation of your mission in your articles of incorporation and the documents filed with the IRS. The downside to formation documents that are too narrowly tailored include a determination that a recurring activity is outside the formation intent and thus taxable. If, by way of example, your partnership program was deemed a merchandising effort outside the purview of the nonprofit mission, it could be entirely taxable, or worse, the entire organization could be deemed a for-profit organization and be treated accordingly. (See IRC Section 513(a).)

KEY PLAYERS

Extremely talented directors are often attracted to nonprofit activities, and they are the least expensive source of talent your organization can obtain. Often they donate their valuable time to help you advance the vision. Who they are and what motivates them may help drive your organizational decisions. Consider electing directors who are outside the culture of your organization and can provide unique insight and talent in their respective disciplines. Then get out of their way and allow them to help you lead. I would much rather hear "no" from a brilliant person than "yes" from a loyal fool. They will also help you recruit other talent, including executive directors and officers.

ENFORCERS

Multiple sets of eyes watch nonprofit activities, including attorneys general in each state, the U.S. Attorney General, state taxing authorities, state departments of corporations, secretaries of state, and the Internal Revenue Service. The results of improper handling of a nonprofit are draconian (exceedingly harsh, severe). Criminal penalties can be imposed for the improper handling of resources or personal inurement transgressions.

Civil penalties can include the determination that the nonprofit is the alter ego of its founder or stakeholders, and thereafter, the tax exempt status can be revoked, thus exposing the stakeholders to back taxes, penalties, and interest calculated back to the date of formation. *Start right, stay right.*

FORMATION VENUE

Form the entity where the bulk of its activities will be conducted. Some who form for-profit entities seek to incorporate where there is no state income tax. This is a distinction without a difference if the activities of that entity are not conducted primarily in that jurisdiction—taxes will be calculated in the state where the business is conducted. Additionally, the jurisdiction of the court where you incorporate will be invoked if you seek legal redress against anyone. Do you want to travel 1,000 miles to obtain relief if someone damages your church? Will your counsel be able to represent you? The answer is "no" unless your attorney is licensed to practice in that state.

Should you form it in another country? The answer to this question transcends the complexity of this text, but suffice it to say that unless you find a reason to incorporate in a jurisdiction that does not have a reciprocal tax treaty with the United States, incorporate domestically.

Common Mistakes

Most businesses, churches included, confuse the credit of the principal with business credit. If you obtain a credit card in the name of your church but you guaranty it, whose credit is damaged when the church fails to make a payment? Yours! Start with a lower credit line (after you obtain a Dunn's number) in the church's name exclusively, pay it off regularly and seek annual increases. Develop the entity's credit independently. Do it now.

Other common mistakes include:

- Using personal credit to finance a business.

- Offering a personal guaranty.

- Applying for loans without first establishing payment history and a business credit score.

- Not being in compliance with the credit bureau requirements.

- Getting red flagged by the business credit bureaus.

- Believing you can repair your business credit alone.

- Believing that federal laws exist to protect against business credit violations by creditors and bureaus.

- Working with vendors who only report negative rather than positive credit experiences.

- Believing business credit is unavailable because of bad personal credit.

- Waiting too long to build business credit.

Would you buy goods from a retailer who red-lined your community? If not, why seek credit from a creditor who refused to report a positive payment history? Would you wait to put a roof on a house until it started to rain? If not, why wait to create a credit profile until you are in desperate need of money and far less bankable?

If you owned two homes and needed one mortgage, would you automatically offer up both properties as collateral? If not, why automatically agree to personally guaranty business credit? Remember, the closed mouth never gets fed. Ask for what you want from creditors. If they refuse, find those who don't.

MINISTRY BUSINESS CREDIT ESTABLISHMENT

In the United States, 90 percent of businesses fail with two years. Why? They run out of cash. The common mistake is the failure to timely establish business credit.

Business Credit

Nine out of ten businesses fail within the first two years because of a lack of cash and credit. Great ideas without adequate capitalization will fail far faster than well-capitalized foolish ones. Enough cash and credit will keep a poorly run company operational forever. Most people, when establishing business credit, fail to seek and obtain the advice of experts and consequently make costly mistakes. The most common mistakes are:

- Using personal credit to finance the business. People form a new corporation and obtain credit cards in the name of their business, thinking, wrongfully, that they are establishing business credit. In fact, they are merely extending and exposing, again, their personal credit.

- Personally guaranteeing business credit. The separate existence of the corporate, or similar form, is designed to shield the stakeholders from personal liability. Why vitiate that protection by personally guarantying debt?

- Applying for business loans prior to the establishment of a business credit rating. Walk, then run. Create the business credit profile first, and then apply for loans. Each inquiry, if they check you as the underlying shareholder, affects your personal credit. Further, maximize your chances for success on the first round, particularly since some credit applications ask, under penalty of perjury, whether you have been declined previously when seeking similar credit.

- Working with vendors who report only negative credit activities. Seek vendors who will report your good credit to the salient bureaus. The world is not short on vendors who will, in addition to taking your money, advance your cause. "Ask and you shall receive."

- Waiting until they need immediate cash to try to create business credit. Establish business credit the moment you open your business. It will be difficult if not impossible to do so after you run out of money and start missing your payment obligations. Remember, good businesses cease to exist because they are under-capitalized. What if you simply missed one order you were depending on, and because of that, you couldn't buy the materials necessary to fill the next order. Now, you are having trouble with your payroll. Your employees are forced to seek alternative employment and you are unable to get a loan to fix it because the creditors reported your company adversely. You lose your business because you failed to arrange a small line of credit to help you manage cash flow before you needed it. Always be prepared.

Church, like any other organization, can create an independent credit profile. Dun & Bradstreet is the central business credit reporting agency. Your church can and should create a profile with Dun & Bradstreet; obtain a Dun's number and use it when seeking credit with financial institutions and others. This process again requires fellowship. This process is inexpensive; and properly executed, you should be able to reduce your cost of funds and expand your organization.

Spend your time engaging in your core business by and through your God-given talents, and allow those skilled in other areas to help advance your vision.

Time to Make Your Vow of Prosperity

We have introduced you to the fundamentals of prosperity and some of the tools necessary to achieve it. Now that you've been led to water, will you drink? God helps those who help themselves. The prison of your current circumstance is not immutable. The keys to the cell remain in your pocket, and you have been introduced to the spiritual solutions for financial freedom.

In future titles, we will explore in more detail real estate investing in any economy, estate planning, the formation and capitalization of your own business, and much more. Your opportunities for prosperity in every sense are as boundless as God's blessings for you. Now that you discovered, at a minimum, your core values of integrity, discipline, knowledge, fellowship, faith, and loyalty, no goal transcends your reach.

Exercise your talents, enjoy His blessings.

Appendix

Appendix

Sample Flash Report

ABC Ministries Flash Report 05/16/2006

Flash Report for the week ending Sunday 5/14/2006

	8:00 AM Pastor Smith Sermon Title 5/14/2006	11:00 AM Elder Davis Sermon Title 5/14/2006	6:00 AM Pastor Smith Sermon Title 1/1/2006	Week Average	05/15/05	Prior Year 5/2/2008 5/15/2005	1/1/2005 5/15/2005	YTD Growth
Income								
Church								
Offerings	7,500	12,000	85,000	4,250	6,750	13,500	121,500	-30%
Tithes	50,000	105,000	553,000	27,650	37,000	70,300	351,500	57%
Building	500	500	4,500	225	-	750	5,500	-18%
Auxiliary	50	85	675	34	27	54	555	22%
Other Income	100	100	1,210	61	-	-	1,000	21%
Subtotal	58,150	117,685	644,385	32,219	43,777	84,604	480,055	34%
Ministry								
Lobby Sales	150	300	1,500	75	100	200	1,200	25%
Bookstore Sales	300	700	4,500	225	275	800	4,200	7%
Internet Sales	700	1,500	10,000	500	-	-	-	0%
Crusade Sales	-	-	12,000	600	500	750	11,000	9%
Partner Program	1,000	1,700	4,700	235	700	1,500	3,900	21%
NSF	-	-	20	1	-	-	1,000	0%
Subtotal	2,150	4,200	32,720	1,636	1,575	3,250	20,300	61%
Total Income	60,300	121,885	677,105	33,855	45,352	87,854	500,355	35%

Bank Accounts

	Bank 5/9/2006	5/16/2006
General	53,000	58,300
Payroll	1,200	1,150
Petty Cash	832	626
Building Fund	7,500	7,500
Designated Funds	5,500	5,500
Ministry	12,000	14,000
	80,032	87,076
Accounts Payable	12,000	17,000

	Week		05/15/05	
Baptisms	5	Prayers	26	
New Members	32	Holy Ghost	1	
Reclaimed	5	Transfers	17	

The bank account balances does not include uncleared checks.

ACTUAL VS. PRIOR COMPARISON

ABC Ministries

Statement of Operations
Actual vs Prior Year

10/28/2005
5:38 PM

	This Year			Last Year			Comparison		
	MTD	QTD	YTD	MTD	QTD	YTD	MTD	QTD	YTD
Combined									
Income									
Church	81,000	187,000	1,286,000	115,950	180,550	913,750	-30%	4%	41%
Ministry	75,000	185,000	520,000	65,500	108,600	640,000	15%	70%	-19%
Total Income	156,000	372,000	1,806,000	181,450	289,150	1,553,750	-14%	29%	16%
Expense									
Church	72,000	173,000	973,000	115,000	212,850	735,000	-37%	-19%	32%
Ministry	83,700	179,151	533,583	41,554	205,000	702,899	101%	-13%	-24%
	155,700	352,151	1,506,583	156,554	417,850	1,437,899	-1%	-16%	5%
Net Income (Loss)	300	19,849	299,417	24,896	(128,700)	115,851	-99%	-115%	158%

Income	Current Year Week	Prior Year Week	Variance
Church			
Offerings	85,000	80,000	6%
Tithes	15,000	18,000	-17%
Auxiliary	5,000	4,500	11%
Building Fund	7,500	-	NA
Other Income	25,000	10,000	150%
Total Income	137,500	112,500	22%
Ministry			
Product	35,000	39,000	-10%
Book Store	105,000	9,500	1005%
Other Income	25,000	30,000	-17%
Total Income	165,000	78,500	110%

Bank Balances	9/27/05
Bank Account 1	105,000
Bank Account 2	175,000
Bank Account 3	15,000
Bank Account 4	2,200
	297,200

Confidential
For Discussion Purposes Only

							Urban Consulting		
Television Sales	10,000	20,000	80,000	35,000	12,000	250,000	-71%	67%	-68%
Other Product	15,000	60,000	225,000	7,000	5,600	30,000	114%	971%	650%
Book Store	50,000	55,000	75,000	2,000	8,000	25,000	2400%	588%	200%
Other Income	-	5,000	15,000	1,500	8,000	35,000	-100%	-38%	-57%
Total Income	75,000	185,000	520,000	65,500	108,600	640,000	15%	70%	-19%
Expense									
Media	40,000	80,000	200,000	25,000	60,000	175,000	60%	33%	14%
Crusades	12,000	24,000	85,000	-	53,000	205,000	NA	-55%	-59%
Fulfillment Center	16,000	24,755	108,288	-	30,000	128,897	NA	-17%	-16%
Book Store	700	5,396	35,295	554	12,000	34,003	26%	-55%	4%
Operations	68,700	134,151	428,583	25,554	155,000	542,899	169%	-13%	-21%
Travel Expense	7,500	22,500	80,000	55,248	275,000	600,000	-86%	-92%	-87%
Sales, Marketing & Admin	15,000	45,000	105,000	16,000	50,000	160,000	-6%	-10%	-34%
Total Expense	83,700	179,151	533,583	41,554	205,000	702,899	101%	-13%	-24%
Net Income (Loss)	(8,700)	5,849	(13,583)	23,946	(96,400)	(62,899)	-136%	-106%	-78%

Confidential
For Discussion Purposes Only

Urban Consulting

ACTUAL VS. BUDGET COMPARISON

ABC Ministries — Statement of Operations — 10/28/2005 5:38 PM

		This Year			Budget			Comparison	
	MTD	QTD	YTD	MTD	QTD	YTD	MTD	QTD	YTD
Church									
Income									
Offerings	15,000	32,000	275,000	15,000	30,000	250,000	0%	7%	10%
Tithes	22,000	25,000	400,000	20,000	60,000	500,000	10%	-58%	-20%
Auxiliary	2,500	12,000	55,000	2,500	7,500	50,000	0%	60%	10%
Building Fund	1,500	40,000	400,000	60,000	70,000	350,000	-98%	-43%	14%
Special Offerings	40,000	78,000	156,000	15,000	45,000	150,000	167%	73%	4%
Total Income	81,000	187,000	1,286,000	112,500	212,500	1,300,000	-28%	-28%	-1%
Expenses									
Payroll	25,000	48,000	144,000	25,000	50,000	112,500	0%	-4%	28%
Utilities	2,000	6,000	15,000	2,500	5,000	11,250	-20%	20%	33%
Total Operational	32,000	63,000	173,000	30,000	60,000	135,000	7%	5%	28%
Auxiliary	8,000	53,000	225,000	30,000	30,000	150,000	-47%	77%	50%
Ministry Expense	25,000	43,000	425,000	50,000	100,000	225,000	-50%	-57%	89%
Pastoral	7,000	14,000	150,000	22,000	44,000	99,000	-68%	-68%	52%
Total Expense	72,000	173,000	973,000	117,000	234,000	609,000	-38%	-26%	60%
Net Ordinary Income (Loss)	9,000	14,000	313,000	(4,500)	(21,500)	691,000	-300%	-165%	-55%
Net Other Income (Expense)	450	450	775	-	1,500	6,500	NA	-70%	-88%
Net Income (Loss)	9,450	14,450	313,775	(4,500)	(20,000)	697,500	-310%	-172%	-55%
Ministry									
Income									
Crusades	-	45,000	125,000	20,000	75,000	300,000	-100%	-40%	-58%
Television Sales	10,000	20,000	80,000	35,000	12,000	250,000	-71%	67%	-68%
Other Product	15,000	60,000	225,000	7,000	5,600	30,000	114%	971%	650%
Book Store	50,000	55,000	75,000	2,000	8,000	25,000	2400%	588%	200%
Other Income	-	5,000	15,000	1,500	8,000	35,000	-100%	-38%	-57%
Total Income	75,000	185,000	520,000	65,500	108,600	640,000	15%	70%	-19%
Expense									
Media	40,000	80,000	200,000	25,000	60,000	175,000	60%	33%	14%
Crusades	12,000	24,000	85,000	-	53,000	205,000	NA	-55%	-59%
Fulfillment Center	16,000	24,755	108,288	-	30,000	128,897	NA	-17%	-16%
Book Store	700	5,396	35,295	554	12,000	34,003	26%	-55%	4%
Operations	68,700	134,151	428,583	25,554	155,000	542,899	169%	-13%	-21%
Travel Expense	7,500	22,500	80,000	55,248	275,000	600,000	-86%	-92%	-87%
Sales, Marketing & Admin	15,000	45,000	105,000	16,000	50,000	160,000	-6%	-10%	-34%
Total Expense	83,700	179,151	533,583	41,554	205,000	702,899	101%	-13%	-24%
Net Income (Loss)	(8,700)	5,849	(13,583)	23,946	(96,400)	(62,899)	-136%	-106%	-78%

Confidential
For Discussion Purposes Only

Urban Consulting

Appendix

ABC Ministries — Statement of Operations — Actual vs Budget — 10/28/2005 5:38 PM

Combined									
Income									
Church	81,000	187,000	1,286,000	112,500	212,500	1,300,000	-28%	-12%	-1%
Ministry	75,000	185,000	520,000	65,500	108,600	640,000	15%	70%	-19%
Total Income	156,000	372,000	1,806,000	178,000	321,100	1,940,000	-12%	16%	-7%
Expense									
Church	72,000	173,000	973,000	117,000	234,000	609,000	-38%	-26%	60%
Ministry	83,700	179,151	533,583	41,554	205,000	702,899	101%	-13%	-24%
	155,700	352,151	1,506,583	158,554	439,000	1,311,899	-2%	-20%	15%
Net Income (Loss)	300	19,849	299,417	19,446	(117,900)	628,101	-98%	-117%	-52%

Confidential — For Discussion Purposes Only — Urban Consulting

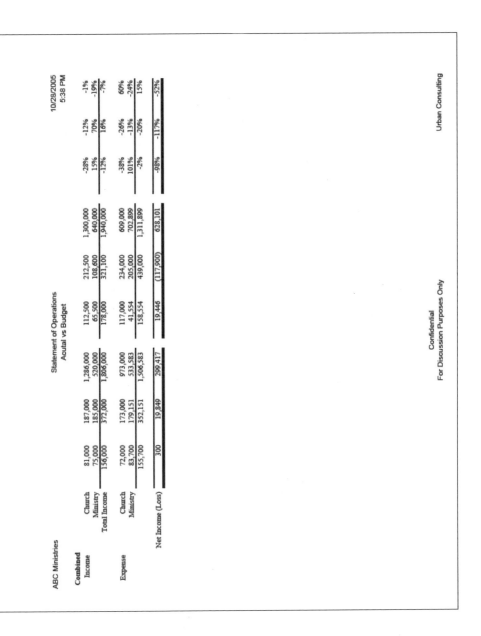

VOW OF PROSPERITY DEFINITIONS

Creativity/Innovation — Thinking outside the box; trying new ways of accomplishing a goal	**Simplicity** — Lack of complexity, complication	**Family** — Being with family, both quality and quantity of time	**Balance** — Balancing time and effort between work, home, hobbies
Independence — Freedom from influence, guidance, or control of others	**Commitment** — Being bound emotionally or intellectually to a course of action, dedication	**Integrity** — Words and deeds match up. I am who I am, no matter where I am or who I am with	**Structure** — Formality, processes and systems
Quality — A standard of excellence	**Volunteerism/Service** — Serving the community, non-profit organizations	**Status** — Holding a position of importance, high standing, prestige	**Fairness** — Treating people and being treated equally
Wisdom — Having deep understanding, insight, and knowledge, the ability to make good judgments	**Teamwork** — Cooperative effort by a group or team	**Perfection** — Reaches the highest attainable standard, details	**Legacy** — Making a difference today with tomorrow in mind, succession
	Growth — Investing in lifelong learning, personal development, self-education	**Urgency** — Fast paced, swift, action oriented	

Appendix

Fitness Being physically fit; optimal well-being	**Fun** Playfulness, ability to laugh and express humor, joking	**Authority** Possessing power over decisions, people, assets	**Accountable** Takes responsibility for both actions and outcomes
Faith/Religion Belief in a higher power	**Trust** Firm reliance on the integrity, ability, or character of a person or thing	**Loyalty** Faithful to a person, an ideal, a custom, a cause, or a duty	**Change** Looking forward to and valuing change, continuous improvement, doing things differently
Money/Wealth An abundance of valuable material possessions, riches	**Passion** Intense emotional excitement, boundless enthusiasm	**Efficiency** Producing results in a timely manner with a minimum of waste, expense, or unnecessary effort	**Achievement** Aspires to the highest levels of excellence
Knowledge Subject matter expert, educated via experience or study	**Competence** Possessing the skill, knowledge and ability to effectively perform	**Recognition** Giving and receiving acknowledgement for achievements	**Diversity** Respecting a variety of cultures/lifestyles
Customer Satisfaction Achieving excellence in customer satisfaction	**Honesty** Being truthful, sincere	**Effectiveness** Executing with precision to achieve results	**Courage** The willingness to take calculated risks and step outside of one's comfort zone

FAITHMATE™
DATING FOR FAITHFUL LIFESTYLES

FaithMate.com is designed for single and previously married urban Christians that are seeking meaningful relationships.

At FaithMate.com, no more uneasy pick-up lines in church. All you need is our PROPRIETARY MATCHING SYSTEM to profile, recommend and connect you with that special someone that the Lord may have just for you.

Find your faith mate today at www.FaithMate.com

When it comes to online dating, all you need is faith, all you need is ...

FAITHMATE™.COM
DATING FOR FAITHFUL LIFESTYLES

Additional copies of this book and other
book titles from Destiny Image are
available at your local bookstore.

Call toll-free: 1-800-722-6774.

Send a request for a catalog to:

Destiny Image® Publishers, Inc.
P.O. Box 310
Shippensburg, PA 17257-0310

*"Speaking to the Purposes of God for This
Generation and for the Generations to Come."*

**For a complete list of our titles,
visit us at www.destinyimage.com.**